KNITTING REIMAGINED

KNITTING REIMAGINED

An Innovative Approach to Structure and Shape with 25 Breathtaking Projects

Nicky Epstein

POTTER
CRAFT

New York

To my husband, Howard, who has
encouraged me to "take the road
less traveled". . . and that *has*
made all the difference!

All rights reserved.
Published in the United States by
Potter Craft, an imprint of Crown
Publishing Group, a division of
Random House LLC, a Penguin
Random House Company, New York.
www.pottercraft.com
www.crownpublishing.com

POTTER CRAFT and colophon is
a registered trademark of Random
House LLC.

Library of Congress Cataloging-in-
Publication Data
Epstein, Nicky.
    Knitting reimagined / Nicky
Epstein.—First edition.
        pages cm
    Includes index.
1. Knitting—Patterns. I. Title.
TT825.E64226 2014
746.43′2—dc23   2013028642

ISBN 978-0-385-34625-2
Ebook ISBN 978-0-385-34626-9

Printed in China

Design by Jan Derevjanik
Photographs by Rose Callahan
Cover design by Jan Derevjanik
Cover photographs by Rose Callahan

The author and publisher would like
to thank the Craft Yarn Council of
America for providing the yarn weight
standards and accompanying icons
used in this book. For more information,
please visit www.YarnStandards.com.

10 9 8 7 6 5 4 3 2 1

First Edition

CONTENTS

INTRODUCTION

I consider *Knitting Reimagined* the destination I've arrived at after a thirty-year journey on a less-traveled road: designing hundreds of published pieces, authoring twenty-five knit and crochet books, and developing and teaching unconventional techniques of knitting. One of my priorities—and passions—over the years has been creating unique designs. I have never adhered to the adage that "everything has been done in knitting." I respect and love traditional knitting techniques, stitches, and patterns, but there comes a time to break new ground, a time for experimentation and improvisation, and a time to rethink and reimagine typical structures and shapes in hand-knitting.

My goal was to fill this book with chic, wearable, but uniquely atypical garments that will appeal to knitters of all skill levels. The stitches are easy, as are the techniques to make the designs, but the resulting structures and shapes are unconventional, unexpected, and, if I do say so myself, showstopping. Hopefully these pieces break interesting new ground in hand-knitting, without being radically over-the-top avant-garde. *Knitting Reimagined* has twenty-five original designs using a variety of forward-looking techniques that will transform your yarn into sophisticated, adaptable knitted garments.

The designs run the gamut from tailored to bohemian, structured to unstructured. They are made with a variety of yarns, including handspun, hand-dyed, novelty, and cashmere. Everything is detailed for you in the instructions and diagrams: stitches, shapes, angles, openings, lengths, button closures, tucks, twists, layering, and more. Also noted are skill levels and approximate time frames to complete each project. You'll find Reimagine It sidebars that offer a few more ideas you can try when knitting the design. Perhaps there will be a suggestion to spark a new idea of your own. What you knit is an expression of yourself, so reimagine what will make each piece uniquely you.

Join me on this road less traveled. I think you'll find it a very surprising and inspiring one.

Happy Knitting,
Nicky

HOW TO USE THIS BOOK

There are three key questions that knitters ask when they choose a project to knit.

1. **Is it hard to make?**
2. **How long does it take to make it?**
3. **How much does the yarn cost?**

Of course, we all vary in our mastery of knitting techniques. We knit with our different experiences, at different speeds, and have different amounts of money that we want to invest. But I've included a general skill level and a ballpark of the amount of time each pattern requires to offer some guidance and give you a frame of reference.

Skill Levels

Beginner friendly: Basic stitches, minimal shaping, simple finishing

Intermediate: More intricate stitches, shaping, and finishing

Advanced: For experienced knitters able to tackle more complicated stitches, shaping, and finishing

Time

Quick: These projects are quick and can be done in a weekend or a few days.

Weeks: These projects take at least a week or more to complete.

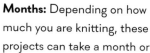

Months: Depending on how much you are knitting, these projects can take a month or more to complete.

chapter 1

DIRECTIONALS

Readers of my book *Knitting Block by Block* already know how creative, easy, and fun it is to combine the simplest shapes and transform them into gorgeous, wearable designs. These directional knits show just a few ways you can construct garments using only rectangles, angles, and squares; think of it as working easy block puzzles. As you can see in the projects in this chapter, the 90-degree corners and angles lend themselves to beautiful draping over the body, but these pieces require little to no shaping. The structure and fit are formed simply by how the shapes are positioned and sewn together!

RECKONING RECTANGLES
shawl

This sheer beauty is a breeze to make with two lush, easy-to-knit rectangles and no additional shaping. Using sequined mohair yarn in a soft lavender adds sparkle and glamour. Knit the edging at the same time, then simply overlap the edgings and sew the rectangles together at the shoulders, leaving a neck opening. The nature-inspired leaf and floral embellishments are appliquéd onto the front lace panel. The rectangles will drape gracefully over the shoulders and flatter all body types.

reimagine it
This wrap can easily be turned into a shrug. Just sew the two rectangles together down the shoulder seam to the wrist, then sew two sleeve seams, leaving a center opening of approximately 22" (56cm). Use any color you like, or try the same idea with a different stitch pattern and embellishment.

SIZE

S/M (L/XL), *shown in S/M*

FINISHED MEASUREMENTS

Each piece measures 12" × 50" (16" × 54") [30.5 × 127 (40.5 × 137)cm]

GAUGE

18 stitches and 24 rows = 4" (10cm) in stitch pattern on smaller needles

Take time to check gauge.

MATERIALS

Skacel Schulana Kid-Paillettes (42% kid mohair, 40% polyester, 18% silk), 0.87oz (25g), 137 yd (125m); 6 (8) balls of #380 Pale Mauve

Size U.S. 7 (4.5mm) straight needles and double-pointed needles, or size needed to obtain gauge

Size U.S. 8 (5mm) straight needles, or one size larger than gauge needles, for casting on and binding off

Tapestry needle

Removable stitch markers

Three 8mm crystal beads for the flower

Open Honeycomb Stitch

(over an odd number of stitches)

Row 1 (RS): Purl.
Row 2: Purl.
Row 3: K1, *yo, ssk; repeat from * to end.
Row 4: Purl.
Repeat rows 1–4 for pattern.

FRONT/BACK (MAKE 2)

With larger needles, cast on 55 (71) stitches.

Change to smaller needles and knit 8 rows.

Next row (RS): K3, work in Open Honeycomb stitch to the last 3 stitches, k3.

Repeat this row, working Open Honeycomb stitch between Garter stitch edges, until piece measures 49 (53)" [124.5 (134.5) cm] from the cast-on edge, ending with row 1.

Knit 8 rows.

Bind off with larger needle.

Note: The stitch pattern will bias; block lightly to shape.

FINISHING

Flower

Cast on 10 stitches with larger needle, leaving a 12" (30.5cm) tail.

Row 1: *Kfb; repeat from * to end—20 stitches.
Row 2: Knit.
Row 3: *Kfb; repeat from * to end—40 stitches.
Row 4: Knit.
Row 5: *K4, kfb; repeat from * to the last 5 stitches, k5—47 stitches.
Rows 6–17: Work in Open Honeycomb stitch.
Row 18: *K2tog; repeat from * to the last stitch, k1—24 stitches.

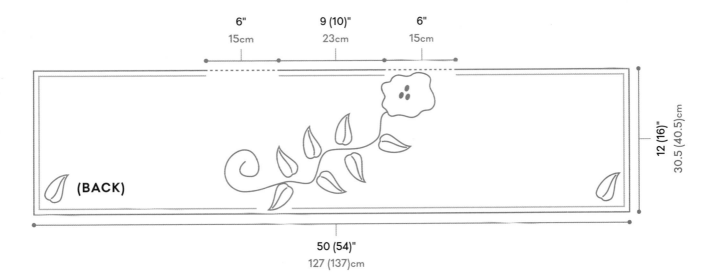

6"
15cm

9 (10)"
23cm

6"
15cm

12 (16)"
30.5 (40.5)cm

(BACK)

50 (54)"
127 (137)cm

Row 19: *K2tog; repeat from * to end—12 stitches.
Row 20: Repeat row 19—6 stitches.
Pass the 2nd, 3rd, 4th, 5th, and 6th stitches, one at a time, over the first stitch and off the needle. Fasten off the last stitch. Weave the tail through the cast-on edge, gather tightly, and secure. Sew the cast-on edge to the bound-off edge to form the Flower and secure. Sew 3 crystal beads to the Flower center.

Leaves (MAKE 9)
Cast on 5 stitches with larger needle.
Row 1 (RS): K2, yo, k1, yo, k2—7 stitches.
Row 2 and all WS rows: Purl.
Row 3: K3, yo, k1, yo, k 3—9 stitches.

Row 5: K4, yo, k1, yo, k4—11 stitches.
Row 7: Knit.
Row 9: Ssk, k7, k2tog—9 stitches.
Row 11: Ssk, k5, k2tog—7 stitches.
Row 13: Ssk, k3, k2tog—5 stitches.
Row 15: Ssk, k1, k2tog—3 stitches.
Row 17: Slip 1, k2tog, psso—1 stitch.
Fasten off.

I-cord
With double-pointed needles, cast on 5 stitches.
*Do not turn. Slide the stitches to the other end of the needle, k5; repeat from * for 17" (43cm).
Next rnd: Do not turn. Slide the stitches to the other end of the needle, k2tog, k1, k2tog—3 stitches.

Last rnd: Do not turn. Slide the stitches to the other end of the needle, k3tog—1 stitch.
Fasten off.

ASSEMBLY
Lay both pieces side by side lengthwise, wrong sides facing up. Mark each side of the center 9 (10)" [23 (25.5)cm] with removable stitch markers for the neck opening. Mark 6" (15cm) out from each neck marker. Overlap the Back garter stitch edge over the Front garter stitch edge from the neck marker to the outer marker for each side, pin in place, and sew securely. The piece drapes over the shoulders and opens at the arms. Sew the Flower, Leaves, and I-cord to the Front using the photo and schematic as a guide. Sew one leaf to the Back.

RENAISSANCE CASTLE
tunic

Featuring an enchanting castle motif, this versatile tunic moves from medieval to modern. Like the Reckoning Rectangles Shawl (page 13) this piece is also created with two rectangles, but with a totally different style. The castle motif is worked using stockinette stitch, reverse stockinette stitch, and seed stitch to create a texture resembling brocade, or relief needle work. Adorned with my castle buttons, the sides are closed at the waist, but of course can be sewn together or left open. This design drapes down the front and back and is crowned with a seed stitch cowl neck and matching buttons.

reimagine it
You can omit the castle, add more colors, and do some bold striping, or, perhaps, sew the side seams, add sleeves, and attach two 10" × 12" (25.5cm × 30.5cm) blocks that can be sewn together to make a hood.

SIZES

S/M (L/XL), *shown in S/M*

FINISHED MEASUREMENTS

Width: 22 (26)" [56 (66)cm]

Length: 29 (30)" [74 (76)cm]

Note: This tunic is worked from the bottom up.

GAUGE

20 stitches and 24 rows = 4" (10cm) in stockinette stitch

Take time to check gauge.

MATERIALS

Cascade Lana D'Oro (50% alpaca, 50% wool), 3½ oz (100g), 219 yd (200m); 4 (5) skeins of #1086 Hare (A), 2 (2) skeins of #1049 Charcoal (B)

Size U.S. 7 (4.5mm) straight needles, or size needed to obtain gauge

Removable stitch markers

Tapestry needle

Three 1⅜" (3.5cm) buttons (JHB's Nicky Epstein Carcassone #92725)

BACK

With B, cast on 110 (130) stitches.

Seed Stitch Edging

Row 1 (RS): *K1, p1; repeat from * to end.

Row 2: *P1, k1; repeat from * to end.

Repeat rows 1 and 2 (seed stitch) for 1½" (3.8cm), ending with a WS row.

Next row (RS): With B, work 7 stitches in seed stitch, join A and k96 (116), join a second ball of B and work the last 7 stitches in seed stitch.

Note: When changing colors, twist yarns on the wrong side to avoid gaps.

Continue working 7 stitches at each end in seed stitch with B and the center 96 (116) stitches in stockinette stitch with A until piece measures 13½" (34.5cm) from the cast-on edge, ending with a WS row.

Mark each end of the next row with removable stitch markers to indicate the button placement.

Next row (RS): Work 7 stitches in seed stitch, k5 (15), work Back chart over the next 86 stitches, k5 (15), work 7 stitches in seed stitch.

Work as established until 58 rows of the Back chart are complete. Continue in seed stitch and stockinette stitch until piece measures 13 (14)" [33 (35.5)cm] from the button markers.

Shape Shoulders

Bind off 1 stitch at the beginning of the next 10 (14) rows, bind off 2 stitches at the beginning of the next 12 (16) rows, then bind off 4 stitches at the beginning of the next 6 (8) rows—52 stitches. Bind off.

Stitch Key

☐ K on RS, P on WS (stockinette stitch)

◼ P on RS, K on WS (reverse stockinette stitch)

Back Chart

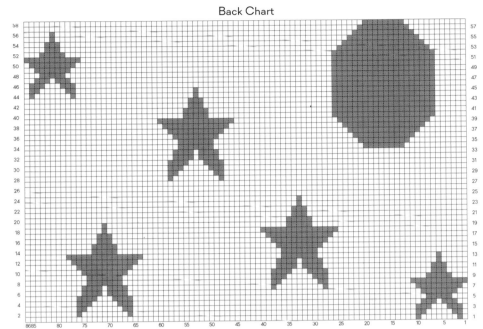

FRONT

Cast on and work Seed Stitch Edging same as for the Back.

Next row (RS): With B, work 7 stitches in seed stitch, join A and k5 (15), work Front chart over the next 86 stitches, k5 (15), join a second ball of B, and work the last 7 stitches in seed stitch.

Note: When changing colors, twist yarns on the wrong side to avoid gaps.

Mark each end for button when it is the same length as back markers.

Work as established until 150 rows of the Front chart are complete.

Piece should measure 26½" (67.5cm) from the cast-on edge.

Shape Shoulders and Neck

Bind off 1 stitch at the beginning of the next 10 (14) rows, bind off 2 stitches at the beginning of the next 12 (16) rows, then bind off 4 stitches at the beginning of the next 6 (8) rows.

At the same time, when 96 stitches remain, shape neck.

Next row (RS): Bind off 2 stitches, k31, join a second ball of A and bind off 30 stitches, knit to the end.

Working on both sides at the same time, continue shaping shoulders as established and work neck shaping as follows:

At each neck edge, bind off 4 stitches twice, then 3 stitches once.

Complete shoulder shaping.

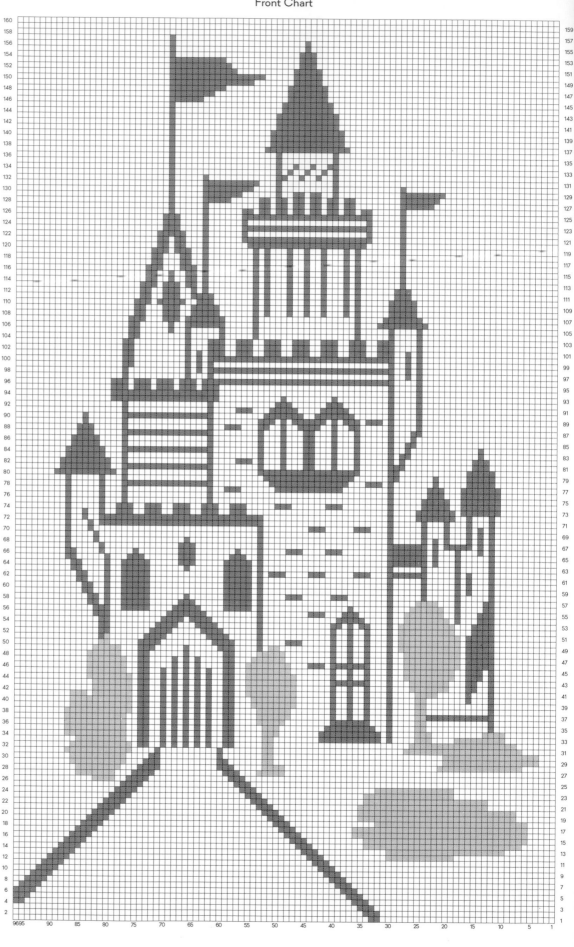

Stitch Key

☐ K on RS, P on WS
   (stockinette stitch)

■ P on RS, K on WS
   (reverse stockinette stitch)

▨ Seed stitch

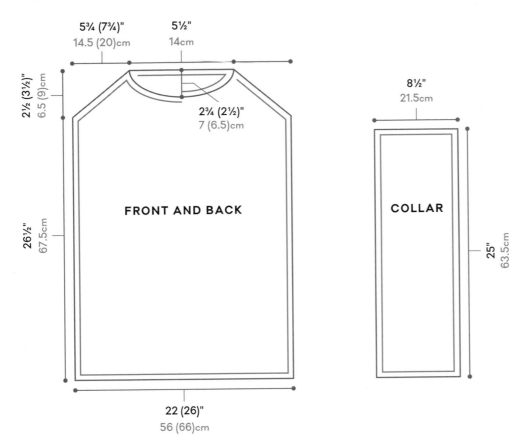

5¾ (7¾)"
14.5 (20)cm

5½"
14cm

2½ (3½)"
6.5 (9)cm

2¾ (2½)"
7 (6.5)cm

FRONT AND BACK

26½"
67.5cm

22 (26)"
56 (66)cm

8½"
21.5cm

COLLAR

25"
63.5cm

FINISHING
Sew shoulder seams.

Collar
With B, cast on 42 stitches. Work in seed stitch for 25" (63.5cm). Bind off.
Place a marker 4" (10cm) down the right front neck from the shoulder seam. Pin the long edge of the collar around the neck opening, working clockwise from the marker and extending the last 4" (10cm) inside the collar to the shoulder seam. Sew in place. Sew a button to the collar overlap as pictured.

Match the Front and Back, overlapping the front seed stitch band over the back band at the button markers. Sew a button at each side through both bands.

ON THE
BLOCK
topper

The topper is quickly becoming a new classic design and is also a favorite
of mine for gift giving. By sewing just four blocks together you can create
an easy cowl or topper. I call this the "magic" topper because it can be
worn multiple ways, has easy sizing and fit, and offers endless design
possibilities. Use any combination of yarns, stitch patterns, and knitted
embellishments. Of course, there are thousands of edgings to choose from
to frame your masterpiece! This design is so satisfying that you will want to
make it over and over for yourself and for others.

reimagine it
The possibilities here are truly endless. You just need
four blocks. They can be any stitch pattern, of one or
many colors, and made with your favorite embellishments
or yarns. For a wealth of block ideas, refer to my book
Knitting Block by Block. It is sure to inspire you. Take a
look at a few examples (page 28) of how to reimage this
design for your own unique style!

SKILL LEVEL

TIME

SIZES

S (M, L, XL), *shown in size S*

FINISHED MEASUREMENTS

Length (including waist and neck ribbing): 19½ (20½, 21½, 22½)" [49.5 (52, 54.5, 57)cm]

Block size: 12 (13, 14, 15)" [30.5 (33, 35.5, 38)cm] square

GAUGE

18 stitches and 24 rows = 4" (10cm) in stockinette stitch on larger needles

Take time to check gauge.

MATERIALS

Cascade Eco Cloud (70% undyed merino wool, 30% undyed alpaca), 3½ oz (100g), 164 yd (150m); 3 (3, 4, 4) balls of #1802 Ecru (A), 3 (3, 4, 4) balls of #1803 Tan (B)

Size U.S. 9 (5.5mm) straight needles, or size needed to obtain gauge

Size U.S. 8 (5mm) 16" (40cm) circular needle

Size U.S. 8 (5mm) 32" (80cm) circular needle

Tapestry needle

Stitch markers

Cable needle

Stitch holders

Piece of cardboard, approximately 11" × 11" (28cm × 28cm)

BLOCKS (MAKE 4, TWO EACH WITH A AND B)

With larger needle, cast on 54 (58, 63, 67) stitches. Work in stockinette stitch until piece measures 12 (13, 14, 15)" [30.5 (33, 35.5, 38)cm]. Bind off. Place 3 blocks side by side, B-A-B, with RS facing up and sew together. (See diagram, page 26.) Flip over so the WS faces up. Place the second A block, RS up,

on top of the first A block. Fold the top edges of the B blocks down to meet the side edges of the second A block, and sew them together.

Bottom Edging

Note: Two markers will be next to each other until rnd 1 is worked. With RS facing, longer circular needle, and color A, and starting at a corner, *pick up and k1 corner stitch, place marker, pick up and k147 (159, 171, 183) stitches evenly to the next corner; place marker; repeat from * once more—296 (320, 344, 368) stitches. Place marker for the beginning of the round, and place marker before corner stitch.

Rnd 1: Slip beginning-of-round marker, [m1p, slip marker, k1, slip marker, m1p, *k3, p3; repeat from * to 3 stitches before the next marker, k3] twice—300 (324, 348, 372) stitches.

Rnd 2: Slip beginning-of-round marker, [p1, m1p, slip marker, k1, slip marker, m1p, p1, *k3, p3; repeat from * to 3 stitches before the next marker, k3] twice. Continue to work edging as established, increasing 1 stitch at each side of the corner stitch and working the increased stitches in purl, until the edging measures 1¼" (3cm). Bind off in rib.

Cable Appliqués (MAKE 2, ONE EACH WITH A AND B)

With larger needle, cast on 12 stitches.

Rows 1 and 3 (WS): K2, p8, k2

Row 2: P2, k8, p2.

Row 4: P2, slip the next 4 stitches to a cn and hold in front, k4, k4 from cn, p2.

Rows 5, 7, and 9: Repeat row 1.

Rows 6, 8, and 10: Repeat row 2.

Repeat rows 1–10 for pattern until piece measures 38 (41, 44, 47)" [96.5 (104, 112, 119.5)cm]. Do not cut yarn. Place stitches on a holder.

COWL

With the RS facing, shorter circular needle, and B, start at a shoulder seam and pick up and k102 (108, 114, 126) stitches evenly around the neck opening. Place marker and join for working in the round.

Work in k3, p3 rib for 2" (5cm). Change to A and continue in rib for 2½" (6.5cm).

Remove marker and work back and forth in rib as established for 1¾" (4.5cm), creating a slit. Bind off in rib.

FINISHING

Place a piece of cardboard inside the garment to keep from sewing the front to the back.

Gather the cast-on edges of the 2 cables and secure.

Pin the cast-on end of cable A to the bottom left corner of one Block A. Lay it diagonally up just past the midpoint of the block and pin in place. Then bring it back to the upper left corner, over the shoulder, diagonally past the midpoint on the second block A, ending back at the lower right corner. Adjust the cable length as needed, and bind off. Repeat for the other cable, working in the opposite direction and looping it under the first cable so that it forms crosses on both front and back. Adjust the cable length as needed, and bind off. Gather the bound-off edges and sew them into a corner seam. Sew the cables in place (see diagram, page 26).

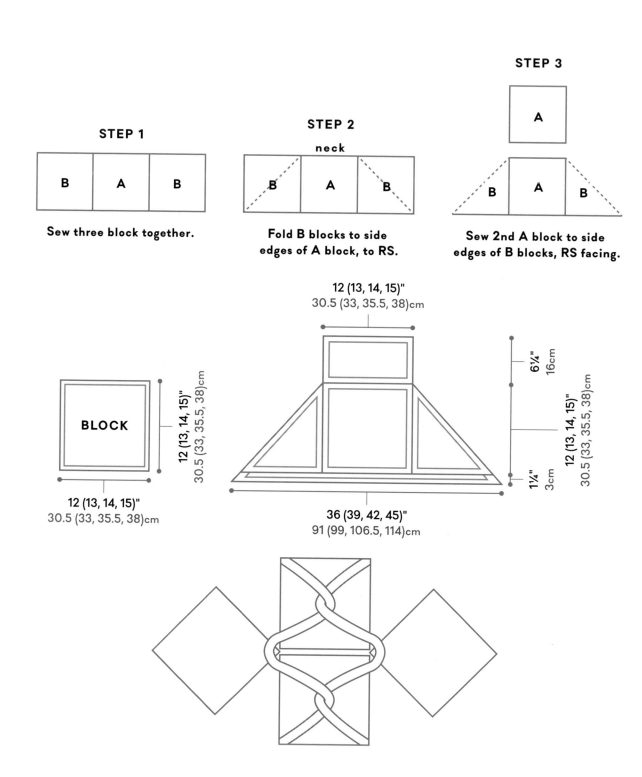

STEP 1

B A B

Sew three block together.

STEP 2

neck

B B A B

Fold B blocks to side
edges of A block, to RS.

STEP 3

A

B A B

Sew 2nd A block to side
edges of B blocks, RS facing.

BLOCK

12 (13, 14, 15)"
30.5 (33, 35.5, 38)cm

12 (13, 14, 15)"
30.5 (33, 35.5, 38)cm

12 (13, 14, 15)"
30.5 (33, 35.5, 38)cm

6¼"
16cm

1¼"
3cm

12 (13, 14, 15)"
30.5 (33, 35.5, 38)cm

36 (39, 42, 45)"
91 (99, 106.5, 114)cm

This is one of my favorite projects to teach because my students learn to think "outside the block" and discover that they can easily make unique designs with just a little imagination. I hope these topper examples will encourage you to reimagine *any* design in this book by simply changing the color, selecting a different stitch pattern, or adding an embellishment.

CLOCKWISE FROM OPPOSITE, TOP LEFT: Garter striping makes lovely angles when the blocks are sewn together; bubble stitch blocks worked in a lovely multicolored yarn, topped with a flower; counterpane lace trimmed with I-cord; multi-cabled blocks with a buttoned edge on one of the seams; a combination of two multi-cable and two plaid blocks topped with a turtleneck and 2×2 mitre edging.

JE NE SAIS QUOI
cape

You will be amazed at how easy and quick this stunning design is to make. Truly one of my designs that looks complex but is not, it is constructed with cleverly placed rectangles and simple stitch pattern repeats that when put together give the design a curved appearance. Notice how the longest rectangles fold in half to create a unique shoulder curve when gathered. The cape is made with a bulky alpaca and large needles for a quick knit that looks like haute couture and is luxurious to wear.

reimagine it
This piece is made in rectangles so you can easily change the stitch patterns, but make sure the yarn is the same weight and gauge to keep the fit. Cuffs can also be added to the arm opening.

TIME

SIZES

S/M (L/XL), *shown in size S/M*

FINISHED MEASUREMENTS

Shoulder width: approximately 15 (18)" [38 (45.5)cm]

Lower edge: 76½ (92)" [194.5 (233.5)cm]

Length: 23 (25)" [58.5 (63.5)cm]

GAUGE

12 stitches and 14 rows = 4" (10cm) in stockinette stitch

Take time to check gauge.

MATERIALS

The BagSmith Blissa Botanicals (85% baby alpaca, 10% extra-fine merino wool, 5% polyamide), 8 oz (226g), 70 yd (64m); 6 (8) balls of Dusty Plum

Size U.S. 15 (10mm) straight needles, or size needed to obtain gauge

Tapestry needle

One 1⅜" (3.5cm) button (JHB's Nicky Epstein Carcassone #92725)

SIDE PANEL (MAKE 2)

Open Rib Stitch
(multiple of 7 stitches + 3)

Cast on 38 (45) stitches.

Row 1 (RS): P3, *k4, p3; repeat from * to end.

Row 2: K1, yo, k2tog, *p4, k1, yo, k2tog; repeat from * to end.

Repeat rows 1 and 2 for pattern.

Work until piece measures 46 (50)" [117 (127)cm].

Bind off.

LEFT FRONT AND COLLAR (MAKE 1)

Elongated Basket Weave
(multiple of 18 stitches + 10)

Cast on 28 stitches.

Row 1 (RS): K11, p2, k2, p2, k11.

Row 2: P1, k8, [p2, k2] twice, p2, k8, p1.

Row 3: K1, p8, [k2, p2] twice, k2, p8, k1.

Row 4: P11, k2, p2, k2, p11.

Rows 5–8: Repeat rows 1–4.

Row 9: Knit.

Row 10: [P2, k2] twice, p12, [k2, p2] twice.

Row 11: [K2, p2] twice, k2, p8, [k2, p2] twice, k2.

Row 12: [P2, k2] twice, p2, k8, [p2, k2] twice, p2.

Row 13: [K2, p2] twice, k12, [p2, k2] twice.

Stitch Key

☐ K on RS, P on WS

⊡ P on RS, K on WS

⊙ Yarn over (yo)

⍁ K2tog on RS; p2tog on WS

☐ Repeat

Open Rib

Elongated Basket Weave

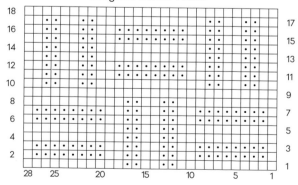

Rows 14–17: Repeat rows 10–13.
Row 18: Purl.
Repeat rows 1–18 for pattern 7 (8) more times. Piece should measure 41½ (46½)" [105.5 (118)cm]. Bind off.

RIGHT FRONT (MAKE 1)

Garter Dash Stitch

(multiple of 10 stitches + 12)
Cast on 32 (42) stitches.
Row 1 (RS): K5, p7, *k4, p6; repeat from * to end.
Rows 2, 4, and 6: Purl to the last 6 stitches, k1, p5.
Row 3: K5, p1, knit to the end.
Row 5: K5, p2, *k4, p6; repeat from * to the last 5 stitches, k5.
Row 7: Repeat row 3.
Row 8: Repeat row 2.
Repeat rows 1–8 for pattern. Work until the piece measures 22 (24)" [56 (61)cm], ending with a WS row.
Buttonhole row 1 (RS): K3, bind off 2 stitches, work in pattern to end.
Buttonhole row 2: Work in pattern to the bound-off stitches, cast on 2 stitches, p3.
Continue in pattern until piece measures 23 (25)" [58.5 (63.5)cm].
Note: The stockinette stitches at the front edge will curl, forming a cord-like edge.

BACK

Seeded Zigzag Stitch

(multiple of 9 stitches)
Cast on 45 (54) stitches.
Row 1 (RS): *[K1, p1] twice, k4, p1; repeat from * to end.
Row 2: *P4, [k1, p1] twice, k1; repeat from * to end.
Row 3: [K1, p1] 3 times, *k4, [p1, k1] twice, p1; repeat from * to the last 3 stitches, k3.
Row 4: P2, *[k1, p1] twice, k1, p4; repeat from * to the last 7 stitches, [k1, p1] twice, k1, p2.
Row 5: K3, *[p1, k1] twice, p1, k4; repeat from * to the last 6 stitches, [p1, k1] 3 times.
Row 6: *[K1, p1] twice, k1, p4; repeat from * to end.
Row 7: Repeat row 5.
Row 8: Repeat row 4.
Row 9: Repeat row 3.
Row 10: Repeat row 2.
Repeat rows 1–10 for pattern. Work until piece measures 19¼ (20¾)" [49 (53)cm].
Continuing in pattern as set, decrease 1 stitch each side every row 13 (15) times—19 (24) stitches.
Bind off.

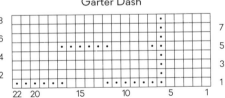

Garter Dash

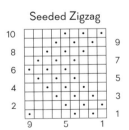

Seeded Zigzag

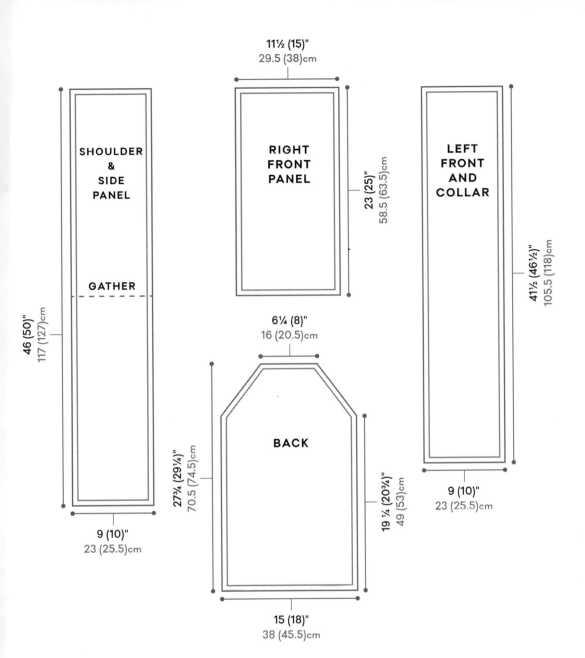

11½ (15)"
29.5 (38)cm

SHOULDER & SIDE PANEL

GATHER

46 (50)"
117 (127)cm

9 (10)"
23 (25.5)cm

RIGHT FRONT PANEL

23 (25)"
58.5 (63.5)cm

6¼ (8)"
16 (20.5)cm

BACK

27¾ (29¼)"
70.5 (74.5)cm

19 ¼ (20¾)"
49 (53)cm

15 (18)"
38 (45.5)cm

LEFT FRONT AND COLLAR

41½ (46½)"
105.5 (118)cm

9 (10)"
23 (25.5)cm

FINISHING

Fold one Side Panel in half with the right sides together. Sew one side of the panel closed, leaving a 6" (15cm) opening approximately 9 (10)" [23 (25.5) cm] from the bottom edge for the armhole. With a doubled length of yarn, tightly gather the open rib stitches across the shoulder line of the panel to 4½ (5)" [11.5 (12.5)cm] and secure to form a nice rounded shoulder. Repeat for the other panel.

Place the Back between the right and left Side Panels, lining it up from the bottom edges to the back neck, and sew in place. The Right Front is sewn to the right Side Panel.

The Left Front is sewn to the left Side Panel, over the left shoulder and across the back neck, over the right shoulder and across the top edge of the Right Front, ending at the p1 stitch of the edging.

Closure

Sew the button to the Left Front, 1" (2.5cm) from the shoulder and the Side Panel, to correspond with the buttonhole.

THE
DEEP END
shawl

This design has a mix of curves, rectangles, and a sharp elongated angle that come together perfectly to create a very unique shawl. There is a bit more knitted construction in this piece, but only two seams connect the three pieces. A cable loop closure is knit into the piece leaving an opening and the deep end point goes through the cable slit to close the shawl. A cable cord edging is knit in on the edges or can be knit separately and sewn around the edges instead. Wear this shawl for a casual elegant look.

reimagine it
I would love to see this stitch pattern made by selecting a solid color for A and a bold variegated yarn for B. Another way to go would be making the two-color stitch pattern with a solid color and then using a contrasting color for the cable slit and cord.

SKILL LEVEL

TIME

SIZES

S/M (L/XL), *shown in size S/M*

FINISHED MEASUREMENTS

Back width: 25¼ (28)" [64.5 (71)cm]

GAUGE

18 stitches and 36 rows = 4" (10cm) in box pattern on larger needles

Take time to check gauge.

MATERIALS

Plymouth Yarn Baby Alpaca Aire (100% baby alpaca), 3½ oz (100g), 218 yd (199m); 2 (3) balls of #5403 Charcoal (A); 5 (6) balls of #5002 Olive (B)

4 MEDIUM

2 pairs of size U.S. 9 (5.5mm) straight needles and a set of 2 double-pointed needles, or size needed to obtain gauge

Size U.S. 2 (2.5mm) 16" (40.5cm) circular needle (or smaller) to hold stitches

Stitch holder

Cable needle

Tapestry needle

1 covered coat hook and eye (optional)

Stitch Key

- A, K on RS, P on WS
- A, P on RS, K on WS
- B, K on RS, P on WS
- B, Slip wyib on RS, Slip wyif on WS
- K on RS, P on WS
- P on RS, K on WS
- 4/4 LC
- 4/4 RC
- Repeat

Box Pattern

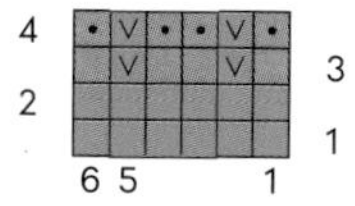

Cables Pattern

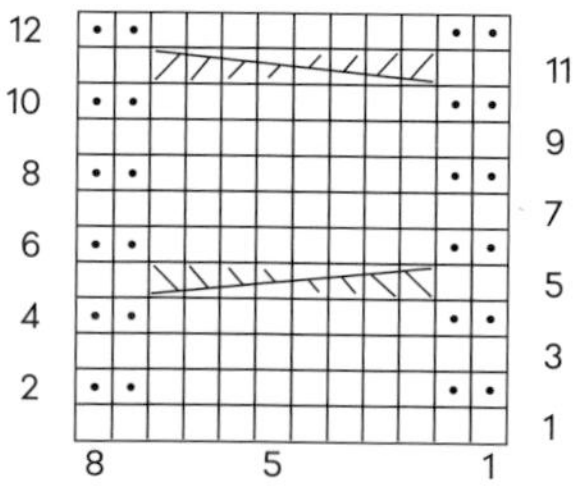

Box Pattern

(multiple of 3 stitches)

Row 1 (RS): With B, knit.

Row 2: With B, purl.

Row 3: With A, k1, slip 1 wyib, *k2, slip 1 wyib; repeat from * to the last stitch, k1.

Row 4: With A, k1, slip 1 wyif, *k2, slip 1 wyif; repeat from * to the last stitch, k1.

Repeat rows 1–4 for pattern.

Cables Pattern

(multiple of 8 stitches)

4/4 RC: Slip 4 stitches to cn and hold in back, k4, k4 from cn.

4/4 LC: Slip 4 stitches to cn and hold in front, k4, k4 from cn.

Row 1 (RS): Knit.

Row 2 and all WS rows: K2, purl to the last 2 stitches, k2.

Row 3: Knit.

Row 5: K2, *4/4 RC; repeat from * to the last 2 stitches, k2.

Rows 7 and 9: Knit.

Row 11: K6, *4/4 LC; repeat from * to the last 6 stitches, k6.

Row 12: Repeat row 2.

Repeat rows 1–12 for pattern.

Cable I-cord

(over 6 stitches)

2/2 LC: Slip 2 stitches to cn and hold in front, k2, k2 from cn.

Rows 1–5: Knit. Do not turn, slide stitches to the other end of the needle.

Row 6: K1, 2/2 LC, k1.
Repeat rows 1–6 for pattern.

BACK

With larger straight needles and B, cast on 114 (126) stitches. Work in Box pattern until piece measures 6¼ (6½)" [16 (16.5) cm], ending with a WS row 4.
Decrease row (RS): K1, ssk, work in Box pattern as established to the last 3 stitches, k2tog, k1.
Repeat Decrease row every 4th row 16 (18) more times—80 (88) stitches.
Work 3 rows even in Box pattern.

Shoulder Shaping

Continuing in Box pattern as established, bind off 6 (7) stitches at the beginning of the next 6 rows—44 (46) stitches.
Bind off.

LEFT FRONT

With larger straight needles and B, cast on 63 (69) stitches. Work in Box pattern until piece measures 14 (15¼)" [35.5 (38.5) cm], ending with a WS row 4.
Next row (RS): Work 46 (48) stitches in Box pattern, insert the smaller circular needle into the front of the last 28 stitches worked and leave it on the RS of

the work to be used later for the Cable Tab, work in Box pattern to end.
Continue in Box pattern for 5" (12.5cm), ending with a WS row 4.
Leave stitches on the needle.

TAB

Place the Tab stitches from the small circular needle onto the second set of larger needles, ready to work a RS row. Join B to the first stitch and work rows 1–12 of Cables pattern for 5" (12.5cm), ending with a WS row.

Join Tab

Return to the Left Front stitches.
Joining row (RS): With B, k18 (20), *knit 1 stitch from the Tab together with 1 stitch from the Left Front; repeat from * until all the Tab stitches have been worked, knit to end—63 (69) stitches.
Continue in Box pattern for 6½" (16.5cm), ending with a WS row 4.

Side Shaping

Next row: Bind off 28 (29) stitches, ssk using the 1 stitch on the right-hand needle as the first stitch, knit to end—34 (39) stitches.

Work 3 rows in Box pattern as established.
Decrease row (RS): K1, ssk, knit to end—33 (38) stitches.
Continuing in Box pattern as established, repeat Decrease row every 4th row 15 (17) more times—18 (21) stitches.
Work 3 rows even in Box pattern as established.

Shoulder Shaping

Bind off 6 (7) stitches at the beginning of the next 3 RS rows.
Fasten off the last stitch.

RIGHT FRONT

With B, cast on 3 stitches.
Row 1 (RS): Knit.
Row 2: Purl.
Row 3: With A, k1, slip 1 wyib, k1.
Row 4: K1, slip 1 wyif, k1.
Row 5: With B, k2, kfb—4 stitches.
Row 6: Purl.
Row 7: With A, k1, slip 1 wyib, k2.

Row 8: K2, slip 1 wyif, k1.

Row 9: With B, k3, kfb—5 stitches.

Row 10: Purl

Row 11: With A, k1, slip 1 wyib, k2, slip 1 wyib.

Row 12: Slip 1 wyif, k2, slip 1 wyif, k1.

Row 13: With B, k4, kfb—6 stitches.

Row 14: Purl.

Row 15: With B, k1, slip 1 wyib, k2, slip 1 wyib, k1.

Row 16: K1, slip 1 wyif, k2, slip 1 wyif, k1.

Continue to increase 1 stitch at the end of every Box pattern row 1 as established until a total of 60 (66) increases have been completed and there are 63 (69) stitches on the needle.

Work 7 rows even in Box pattern, ending with a WS row 4.

Next Row (RS): With B, k33 (38), k2tog, k28 (29).

Side Shaping

Next row (WS): Bind off 28 (29) stitches, purl to end—34 (39) stitches.

Work Box pattern rows 3 and 4 as established.

Decrease row (RS): With B, knit to the last 3 stitches, k2tog, k1—33 (38) stitches.

Continuing in Box pattern as

established, repeat Decrease row every 4th row 15 (17) more times—18 (21) stitches.

Work 4 rows even in Box pattern as established.

Shoulder Shaping

Bind off 6 (7) stitches at the beginning of the next 3 WS rows. Fasten off.

FINISHING

With the RS together, sew the 28 (29) bound-off stitches of the fronts to the side edges of the Back, the decrease edges and shoulder bind-offs, one after the other, as one seam.

Cable I-cord Trim

With dpns and a doubled strand of B, cast on 6 stitches. With the RS facing, start across the cast-on edge of the Left Front.

Joining row: K5, slip 1, pick up and k1 stitch, psso.

Repeat the Joining row, working rows 1–6 of Cable I-cord, picking up and attaching 1 stitch on the body of the shawl for each I-cord row. When all cast-on stitches have been worked, work 5 rows of Cable I-cord without attaching them, for the corner.

Continue to work Cable I-cord, attaching it evenly (approximately

every 3rd row) up the side edge of the Left Front, across the Back, down the side edge of the Right Front, and around the front edges back to the start, working 5 unattached rows at each corner. Use the Kitchener stitch (see page 170) to graft the 2 ends together. Sew hook and eye (optional) at V-point on each side, under the cable edge where the fronts cross.

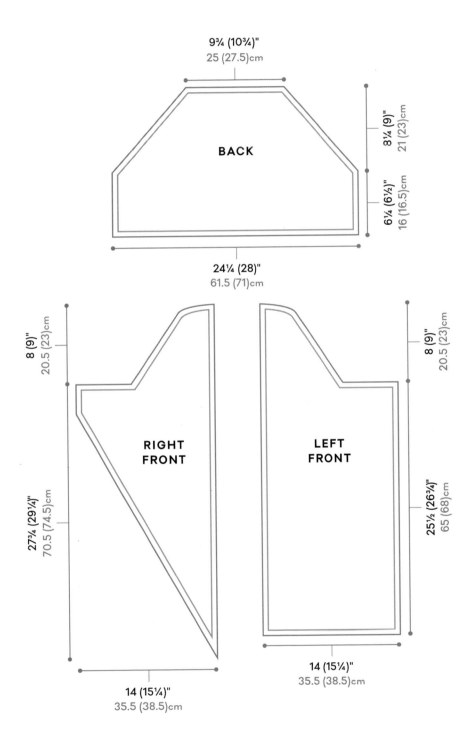

9¾ (10¾)"
25 (27.5)cm

BACK

8¼ (9)"
21 (23)cm

6¼ (6½)"
16 (16.5)cm

24¼ (28)"
61.5 (71)cm

8 (9)"
20.5 (23)cm

RIGHT FRONT

LEFT FRONT

8 (9)"
20.5 (23)cm

27¾ (29¼)"
70.5 (74.5)cm

25½ (26¾)"
65 (68)cm

14 (15¼)"
35.5 (38.5)cm

14 (15¼)"
35.5 (38.5)cm

ROYAL LACE
coat with hood

Like something out of a fairy tale, this design is created by sewing seven rectangles together and adding a detachable hood. Each rectangle is made with graduated arrow lace that knits up like a dream and converges into stockinette stitch forming lovely lace points on all the rectangles. The sleeves add structure for a more tailored fit, and the shape is perfectly flattering for any body size. Always in style, it's a piece that should be in everyone's closet. The sample pictured uses my Knight's Amour buttons and Fleur de Lis clasp from JHB.

reimagine it
Keep the lace pattern and construction, but try using a fabulous subtly colored, hand-dyed yarn. Add a different button and closure choice for a completely new look.

SKILL LEVEL

TIME

SIZES

S/M (L/XL), *shown in size L/XL*

FINISHED MEASUREMENTS

Bust: 39½ (47½)" [100 (120.5) cm]

Length: 23¼ (25)" [59 (63.5)cm]

GAUGE

16 stitches and 24 rows = 4" (10cm) in stockinette stitch on larger needles

Take time to check gauge.

MATERIALS

Cascade Cloud (70% merino wool, 30% baby alpaca), 3½ oz (100g), 164 yd (150m); 8 (9) skeins of #2109 Red

Size U.S. 10 (6mm) needles, or size needed to obtain gauge

Size U.S. 9 (5.5mm) needles

Stitch markers

Stitch holders

Tapestry needle

Six 1⅛" (2.8cm) buttons (JHB's Nicky Epstein Knight's Armour #92723)

1 clasp (JHB's Nicky Epstein Fleur de Lis #4042)

Row 3: K1, *yo, ssk, k3, k2tog, yo, k1; repeat from * to end.
Row 4: P2, *yo, p2tog, p1, p2tog tbl, yo, p3; repeat from * to the last 7 stitches, yo, p2tog, p1, p2tog tbl, yo, p2.
Row 5: K3, *yo, s2kp, yo, k5; repeat from * to the last 6 stitches, yo, s2kp, yo, k3.
Row 6: Repeat row 2.
Row 7: Repeat row 1.
Row 8: P1, *yo, p2tog, p3, p2tog tbl, yo, p1; repeat from * to end.
Row 9: K2, *yo, ssk, k1, k2tog, yo, k3; repeat from * to the last 7 stitches, yo, ssk, k1, k2tog, yo, k2.
Row 10: P3, *yo, s2pp, yo, p5; repeat from * to the last 6 stitches, yo, s2pp, yo, p3.
Repeat rows 1–10 for pattern.

Pattern 2
(multiple of 8 stitches +1)
Rows 1 and 3: K1, *ssk, [k1, yo] twice, k1, k2tog, k1; repeat from * to end.
Row 2 and all WS rows: Purl.
Row 5: K1, *yo, ssk, k3, k2tog, yo, k1; repeat from * to end.
Row 7: K2, *yo, ssk, k1, k2tog, yo, k3; repeat from * to the last 7 stitches, yo, ssk, k1, k2tog, yo, k2.
Row 9: K3, *yo, s2kp, yo, k5; repeat from * to the last 6 stitches, yo, s2kp, yo, k3.
Row 10: Purl.
Repeat rows 1–10 for pattern.

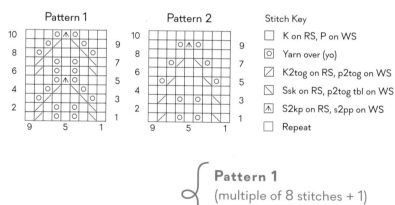

Pattern 1   Pattern 2   Stitch Key
□ K on RS, P on WS
⊡ Yarn over (yo)
⊠ K2tog on RS, p2tog on WS
⧅ Ssk on RS, p2tog tbl on WS
⋏ S2kp on RS, s2pp on WS
□ Repeat

Pattern 1
(multiple of 8 stitches + 1)
Row 1 (RS): K1, *ssk, [k1, yo] twice, k1, k2tog, k1; repeat from * to end.
Row 2: P1, *p2tog, [p1, yo] twice, p1, p2tog tbl, p1; repeat from * to end.

BACK

With larger needles, cast on 85 (101) stitches.

Knit 2 rows.

Row 1 (RS): [K1, p1] 3 times, place marker, work 73 (89) stitches in Pattern 1, place marker, [p1, k1] 3 times.

Rows 2–70: Keeping 6 stitches at each end in rib as set, work Pattern 1 rows 2–10 between markers once, then work rows 1–10 another 6 times.

Row 71: [K1, p1] 3 times, slip marker, work 73 (89) stitches in Pattern 2, slip marker, [p1, k1] 3 times.

Rows 72–80: Keeping 6 stitches at each end in rib as established, work Pattern 2 rows 2–10 between markers.

Row 81: [K1, p1] 3 times, remove marker, k8, place marker, work 57 (73) stitches in Pattern 2 as established, place marker, k8, remove marker, [p1, k1] 3 times.

Rows 82–90: Work 6 stitches in rib, 8 stitches in stockinette stitch, Pattern 2 rows 2–10 between markers, 8 stitches in stockinette stitch, and the last 6 stitches in rib.

Row 91: [K1, p1] 3 times, k8, remove marker, k8, place marker, work 41 (57) stitches in Pattern 2 as established, place marker, k8, remove marker, k8, [p1, k1] 3 times.

Rows 92–100: Work 6 stitches in rib, 16 stitches in stockinette stitch, Pattern 2 rows 2–10 between markers, 16 stitches in stockinette stitch, and the last 6 stitches in rib.

Row 101: [K1, p1] 3 times, k16, remove marker, k8, place marker, work 25 (41) stitches in Pattern 2 as established, place marker, k8, remove marker, k16, [p1, k1] 3 times.

Rows 102–110: Work 6 stitches in rib, 24 stitches in stockinette stitch, Pattern 2 rows 2–10 between markers, 24 stitches in stockinette stitch, and the last 6 stitches in rib.

Row 111: [K1, p1] 3 times, k24, remove marker, k8, place marker, work 9 (25) stitches in Pattern 2 as established, place marker, k8, remove marker, k24, [p1, k1] 3 times.

Rows 112–120: Work 6 stitches in rib, 32 stitches in stockinette stitch, Pattern 2 rows 2–10 between markers, 32 stitches in stockinette stitch, and the last 6 stitches in rib.

Size S/M only, skip to row 131.

Row 121: [K1, p1] 3 times, k32, remove marker, k8, place marker, work 9 stitches in Pattern 2 as established, place marker, k8, remove marker, k32, [p1, k1] 3 times.

Rows 122–130: Work 6 stitches in rib, 40 stitches in stockinette stitch, Pattern 2 rows 2–10 between markers, 40 stitches in stockinette stitch, and the last 6 stitches in rib.

Rows 131–150: Work 6 stitches in rib, 73 (89) stitches in stockinette stitch (remove markers on row 131), and the last 6 stitches in rib. Place stitches on a holder.

LEFT FRONT

With larger needles, cast on 45 (53) stitches.

Knit 2 rows.

Row 1: [K1, p1] 3 times, place marker, work 33 (41) stitches in Pattern 1, place marker, [p1, k1] 3 times.

Rows 2–10: Work 6 stitches in rib, slip marker, work Pattern 1 rows 2–10 between markers, slip marker, work the last 6 stitches in rib.

Rows 11–70: Repeat rows 1–10 six more times.

Row 71: [K1, p1] 3 times, slip marker, work 33 (41) stitches in Pattern 2, slip marker, [p1, k1] 3 times.

Rows 72–80: Work 6 stitches in rib, Pattern 2 rows 2–10 between markers, and the last 6 stitches in rib.

Row 81: [K1, p1] 3 times, remove marker, k8, place marker, work 25 (33) stitches in Pattern 2, slip marker, [p1, k1] 3 times.

Rows 82–90: Working rib and stockinette stitches as set, work Pattern 2 rows 2–10 between markers.

Row 91: [K1, p1] 3 times, k8, remove marker, k8, place marker, work 17 (25) stitches in Pattern 2, slip marker, [p1, k1] 3 times.

Rows 92–100: Working rib and stockinette stitches as set, work Pattern 2 rows 2–10 between markers.

Row 101: [K1, p1] 3 times, k16,

remove marker, k8, place marker, work 9 (17) stitches in Pattern 2, slip marker, [p1, k1] 3 times.

Rows 102–110: Working rib and stockinette stitches as set, work Pattern 2 rows 2–10 between markers.

Size S/M only, skip to row 121.

Row 111: [K1, p1] 3 times, k24, remove marker, k8, place marker, work 9 stitches in Pattern 2, slip marker, [p1, k1] 3 times.

Rows 112–120: Working rib and stockinette stitches as set, work Pattern 2 rows 2–10 between markers.

Rows 121–139: Work in rib stitches as set and 33 (41) stitches between markers in stockinette stitch.

Neck

Bind off 8 (10) stitches at beginning of next WS row. Continue to bind off at the beginning of WS rows, 3 (4) stitches twice, and 2 stitches 3 times. Place the remaining 25 (29) stitches on a holder.

RIGHT FRONT

With larger needles, cast on 45 (53) stitches.

Knit 2 rows.

Row 1: [K1, p1] 3 times, place marker, work 33 (41) stitches in

Pattern 1, place marker, [p1, k1] 3 times.

Rows 2–10: Work 6 stitches in rib, work Pattern 1 rows 2–10 between markers, work the last 6 stitches in rib.

Rows 11–70: Repeat rows 1–10 6 more times.

Row 71: [K1, p1] 3 times, slip marker, work 33 (41) stitches in Pattern 2, slip marker, [p1, k1] 3 times.

Rows 72–80: Work 6 stitches in rib, Pattern 2 rows 2–10 between markers, and the last 6 stitches in rib.

Row 81: [K1, p1] 3 times, slip marker, work 25 (33) stitches in Pattern 2, place marker, k8, remove marker, [p1, k1] 3 times.

Rows 82–90: Working rib and stockinette stitches as set, work Pattern 2 rows 2–10 between markers.

Row 91: [K1, p1] 3 times, slip marker, work 17 (25) stitches in Pattern 2, place marker, k8, remove marker, k8, [p1, k1] 3 times.

Rows 92–100: Working rib and stockinette stitches as set, work Pattern 2 rows 2–10 between markers.

Row 101: [K1, p1] 3 times, slip marker, work 9 (17) stitches in Pattern 2, place marker, k8, remove marker, k16, [p1, k1] 3 times.

Rows 102–110: Working rib and stockinette stitches as set, work Pattern 2 rows 2–10 between markers.

Size S/M only, skip to row 121.

Row 111: [K1, p1] 3 times, slip marker, work 9 stitches in Pattern 2, place marker, k8, remove marker, k24, [p1, k1] 3 times.

Rows 112–120: Working rib and stockinette stitches as set, work Pattern 2 rows 2–10 between markers.

Rows 121–138: Work in rib stitches as set and 33 (41) stitches between ribs in stockinette stitch.

Neck

Bind off 8 (10) stitches at beginning of next RS row. Continue to bind off at the beginning of RS rows, 3 (4) stitches twice, and 2 stitches 3 times. Place the remaining 25 (29) stitches on a holder.

SLEEVES (MAKE 2)

With larger needles, cast on 43 stitches.

Knit 2 rows.

Row 1: K1, place marker, work 41 stitches in Pattern 1, place marker, k1.

Rows 2–14: Keeping the first and last stitches in stockinette stitch, work Pattern 2 rows 2–10 then rows 1–4 between markers.

Row 15 (increase row): K1, m1, slip marker, work Pattern 2 row 5 between markers, slip marker, m1, k1.

Repeat increase row every 6th row 8 (10) more times, working m1 one stitch in from each edge, working increases in stockinette stitch as follows:

Rows 16–20: Keeping the first 2 and last 2 stitches in stockinette stitch, work Pattern 2 rows 6–10 between markers.

Row 21 (increase row): K1, m1, k1, remove marker, k8, place marker, work 25 stitches in Pattern 2, place marker, k8, remove marker, k1, m1, k1.

Rows 22–30: Keeping stitches at each end in stockinette stitch, work Pattern 2 rows 2–10 between markers—49 stitches. (Row 27 is an increase row.)

Row 31: K12, remove marker, k8, place marker, work 9 stitches in Pattern 2, place marker, k8 remove marker, k12.

Rows 32–40: Working stitches at each end in stockinette stitch, work Pattern 2 rows 2–10 between markers—53 stitches. (Rows 33 and 39 are increase rows.)

Row 41: Knit across, removing markers.

Continue in stockinette stitch, increasing as established, until you have 61 (65) stitches. If necessary, work even in stockinette stitch until Sleeve measures 16" (40.5cm) from the cast-on edge, or to desired length.

Bind off.

HOOD

RIGHT SIDE

Bottom Edge

Cast on 40 (48) stitches with larger needles.

Work in knit 1, p1 for a total of 9 rows.

Body

Row 1 (RS): [K1, p1] 3 times, place marker, work 33 (41) stitches in Pattern 2, place marker, k1.

Rows 2–10: Work rib stitches as set, work Pattern 2 rows 2–10 between markers.

Row 11: [K1, p1] 3 times, slip marker, work 25 (33) stitches in Pattern 2, place marker, k8, remove marker, k1.

Rows 12–20: Work rib and stockinette stitches as set, work Pattern 2 rows 2–10 between markers.

Row 21: [K1, p1] 3 times, slip marker, work 17 (25) stitches in Pattern 2, place marker, k8, remove marker, k9.

Rows 22–30: Work rib and stockinette stitches as set, work Pattern 2 rows 2–10 between markers.

Row 31: [K1, p1] 3 times, slip marker, work 9 (17) stitches in Pattern 2, place marker, k8, remove marker, k17.

Rows 32–40: Work rib and stockinette stitches as set, work Pattern 2 rows 2–10 between markers.

Row 41: [K1, p1] 3 times, slip marker, work 0 (9) stitches in Pattern 2, place marker, k8, remove marker, k25.

Rows 42–50: Work rib and stockinette stitches as set; *for size L/XL only,* work Pattern 2 rows 2–10 between the markers.

Row 51: [K1, p1] 3 times, knit to end, removing all markers.

Row 52: Purl to the last 6 stitches, [k1, p1] 3 times.

Repeat rows 51 and 52 until Hood measures 12" (30.5cm) from the cast-on edge, ending with a WS row.

Bind off.

LEFT SIDE
Bottom Edge
With larger needles, cast on 40 (48).

Starting on the WS, work k1, p1 for a total of 9 rows.

Body
Row 1 (RS): K1, place marker, work 33 (41) stitches in Pattern 2, place marker, [p1, k1] 3 times.

Rows 2–10: Work rib stitches as set, work Pattern 2 rows 2–10 between markers.

Row 11: K1, remove marker, k8, place marker, work 25 (33) stitches in Pattern 2, slip marker, [p1, k1] 3 times.

Rows 12–20: Work rib and stockinette stitches as set, work Pattern 2 rows 2–10 between markers.

Row 21: K9, remove marker, k8, place marker, work 17 (25) stitches in Pattern 2, slip marker, [p1, k1] 3 times.

Rows 22–30: Work rib and stockinette stitches as set, work Pattern 2 rows 2–10 between markers.

Row 31: K17, remove marker, k8, place marker, work 9 (17) stitches in Pattern 2, slip marker, [p1, k1] 3 times.

Rows 32–40: Work rib and stockinette stitches as set, work Pattern 2 rows 2–10 between markers.

Row 41: K25, remove marker, work 0 (9) stitches in Pattern 2, slip marker, [p1, k1] 3 times.

Rows 42–50: Work rib and stockinette stitches as set; *for size L/XL only,* work Pattern 2 rows 2–10 between markers.

Row 51: Knit to the last 6 stitches, [p1, k1] 3 times, removing all markers.

Row 52: [P1, k1] 3 times, purl to end.

Repeat rows 51 and 52 until Hood measures 12" (30.5cm) from the cast-on edge, ending with a WS row.

Bind off.

FINISHING
With the right sides together, use the 3-needle bind-off (see page 169) to join the shoulders, leaving the 35 (43) Back neck stitches on a holder.

Neck Band
With RS facing and smaller needles, pick up and k21 (25) stitches from Right Front neck edge to the right shoulder seam; k35 (43) Back neck stitches, increasing 2 stitches evenly across [37 (45) stitches]; pick up and k21 (25) stitches from the left shoulder seam down to the Left Front edge—79 (95) stitches.

Row 1 (WS): P1, *k1, p1; repeat from * to end.

Row 2: K1, *p1, k1; repeat from * to end.

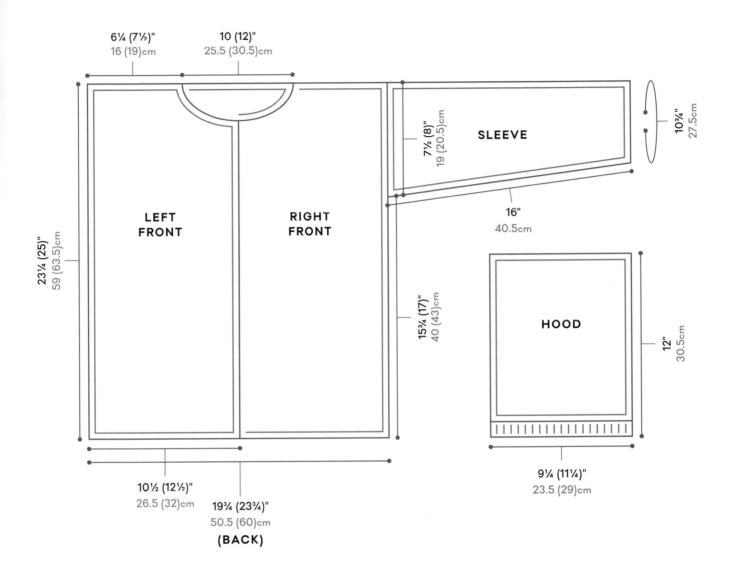

6¼ (7½)"
16 (19)cm

10 (12)"
25.5 (30.5)cm

7½ (8)"
19 (20.5)cm

SLEEVE

10¾"
27.5cm

LEFT FRONT

RIGHT FRONT

23¼ (25)"
59 (63.5)cm

16"
40.5cm

15¾ (17)"
40 (43)cm

HOOD

12"
30.5cm

10½ (12½)"
26.5 (32)cm

19¾ (23¾)"
50.5 (60)cm

(BACK)

9¼ (11¼)"
23.5 (29)cm

MAKE BUTTONHOLES

Row 3: Rib 3, [bind off 3 stitches, rib 11 (14)] twice, bind off 3 stitches, rib 11 (15), [bind off 3 stitches, rib 11 (14)] twice, bind off 3 stitches, rib 3.

Row 4: Work in rib, casting on 3 stitches over the bound-off stitches.

Continue to work in rib until band measures 1½" (3.8cm). Bind off in rib.

Reinforce buttonholes with whipstitch (see page 171). Measure and mark 7½ (8)" [19 (20.5)cm] down from the shoulder on both the back and the front. Sew Sleeves between the markers under the rib edging (see photograph). Sew sleeve seams. With the right sides together, sew the top and back seams of the Hood. Sew buttons onto the

Hood to correspond with the neck-band buttonholes. Sew the clasp to the front at the neck (see photograph, page 43).

WELTED
BUTTON
tuck cardi

This asymmetrical style has an unusual drape and shape, and traditional armhole shaping for fit. The multiple buttons and buttonholes do much of the work by creating graceful folds and flowing tucks. The two front shapes are completely different, but when tucked at the sides and sewn into the back it creates a perfect fit. The sleeve cuffs have a little ruching and each is topped with a button. You need to enjoy the stockinette stitch because there is a lot of it! It is the perfect piece for therapeutic, stress-free, or on-the-go knitting.

reimagine it
Multicolored dyed yarns often create a one-of-a-kind look, such as the diamond patterning on the back. Yours may end up on the front! Try keeping the welted button side in one color, with the other side in two-color striping and the sleeves in another color. Consider adding a pocket to the left side.

TIME

SIZES

S/M (L/XL), *shown in size S/M*

FINISHED MEASUREMENTS

Bust: 39 (50½)" [99 (128)cm]

Back length: 32½ (34½)" [82.5 (87.5)cm] at back point edge

Sleeve length 20" (51cm) before gather

Note: The front and back of this sweater are made from the top down. The sleeves are worked from the cuff up. The sleeves are intentionally long.

GAUGE

20 stitches and 24 rows = 4" (10cm) in stockinette stitch

Take time to check gauge.

MATERIALS

Blue Heron Yarns Rayon Metallic (88% rayon, 12% metallic), 8 oz (226g), 550 yd (503m); 3 (4) skeins of Water Hyacinth

Size U.S. 7 (4.5mm) straight needles, or size needed to obtain gauge

Tapestry needle

Eleven ¾" (2cm) buttons (JHB's Feng Shui #96992)

BACK

Cast on 83 (90) stitches.

Rows 1–45 (1–35): Starting with a purl row, work 45 (35) rows in stockinette stitch.

Armhole Shaping

Row 46 (36) (RS): K1, m1, knit to the last stitch, m1, k1—85 (92) stitches.

Row 47 (37): Purl.

Rows 48–51 (38–55): Repeat rows 46 and 47 twice (rows 36 and 37 nine times)—89 (110) stitches.

Row 52 (56): Cast on 4 (8) stitches, knit to the end—93 (118) stitches.

Row 53 (57): Cast on 4 (8) stitches, purl to the end—97 (126) stitches.

Rows 54–71 (58–75): Work 18 rows in stockinette stitch.

Row 72 (76): K1, m1, knit to the last stitch, m1, k1—99 (128) stitches.

Rows 73–89 (77–93): Work 17 rows in stockinette stitch.

Rows 90–143 (94–147): Repeat rows 72–89 (76–93) 3 times—105 (134) stitches. Work even in stockinette stitch until piece measures 16" (40.5cm) from the underarm, ending with a RS row.

Shape Lower Edge

Rows 1, 3, and 5 (WS): Purl.

Row 2: Bind off 5 stitches, knit to the end—100 (129) stitches.

Rows 4 and 6: Bind off 4 stitches, knit to the end—92 (121) stitches.

Rows 7–48 (7–54): Repeat rows 1–6 seven more times (rows 1 and 2 twenty-four times).

Fasten off the last stitch.

RIGHT FRONT

Cast on 14 (18) stitches.

Row 1 (WS): Purl.

Neck Shaping

Row 2: Knit to the last stitch, m1, k1—15 (19) stitches.

Rows 3–24: Repeat rows 1 and 2 eleven more times—26 (30) stitches.

Rows 25 and 27: Purl.

Row 26: Knit.

Row 28: Knit to the last stitch, m1, k1—27 (31) stitches.

Rows 29–44 (29–34): Repeat rows 27 and 28 eight (three) more times—35 (34) stitches.

Row 45 (35): Purl.

Armhole Shaping

Row 46 (36): K1, m1, knit to the last stitch, m1, k1—37 (36) stitches.

Row 47 (37): Purl.

Rows 48–51 (38–55): Repeat rows 46 and 47 twice (36 and 37 nine times)—41 (54) stitches.

Row 52 (56): Cast on 4 (8) stitches, knit to the last stitch, m1, k1—46 (63) stitches.

Rows 53 and 55 (57 and 59): Purl.

Row 54 (58): Knit.

Row 56 (60): Knit to the last stitch, m1, k1—47 (64) stitches.

Rows 57–244 (61–256): Repeat rows 1–28 six (seven) more times, then rows 1–20 once (zero times) more—135 (155) stitches.

Row 245 (257): Purl.

Row 246 (258): Bind off 5

stitches, knit to the last stitch, m1, k1—131 (151) stitches.

Rows 247–268 (259–280): Repeat rows 245 and 246 (257–258) eleven times—87 (107) stitches.

Row 269 (281): Purl.

Row 270 (282): Bind off 5 stitches, knit to end—82 (102) stitches.

Rows 271 (283): Purl.

Row 272 (284): Bind off 5 stitches, knit to the last stitch, m1, k1—78 (98) stitches.

Rows 273–300 (285–312): Repeat rows 245–272 (257–284) once—21 (41) stitches.

Rows 301–310 (313–332): Repeat rows 271 and 272 five times (271–272 ten times). Fasten off the last stitch.

LEFT FRONT

Cast on 14 (18) stitches.

Row 1 (WS): Purl.

Neck Shaping

Row 2: K1, m1, knit to the end—15 (19) stitches.

Rows 3–44 (3–34): Repeat rows 1 and 2 twenty-one (sixteen) more times—36 (35) stitches.

Row 45 (35): Purl.

Armhole Shaping

Row 46 (36): K1, m1, knit to the last stitch, m1, k1—38 (37) stitches.

Rows 47–50 (37–54): Repeat rows 45 and 46 twice (nine times)—42 (55) stitches.

Row 51 (55): Cast on 4 (8) stitches, purl to the end—46 (63) stitches.

Row 52 (56): K1, m1, knit to the end—47 (64) stitches.

Row 53 (57): Purl.

Rows 54–71 (58–79): Repeat rows 52 and 53 nine more times (56 and 57 eleven more times)—56 (75) stitches.

Work even in stockinette stitch until piece measures 16" (40.5cm) from the underarm, ending with a WS row.

Shape Lower Edge

Row 1 (RS): Knit.

Row 2: Bind off 6 stitches, purl to the end—50 (69) stitches.

Row 3: Knit.

Row 4: Bind off 5 stitches, purl to the end—45 (64) stitches.

Rows 5–19 (21): Repeat rows 1–4 four (five) more times; *for size L/XL only*, work rows 1 and 2 once more.

For size S/M, fasten off the last stitch; *for size L/XL*, bind off the remaining 3 stitches.

SLEEVES

Cast on 45 (51) stitches.

Knit 4 rows.

Starting with a purl row, work in stockinette stitch for 4" (10cm), ending with a WS row.

Increase row (RS): K1, m1, knit to the last stitch, m1,k1.

Continuing in stockinette stitch, repeat Increase row every 4th row 2 (19) more times, then every 6th row 11 (0) times—73 (91) stitches.

Work even until piece measures 20" (51cm) from cast-on or to desired length, ending with a WS row.

Cap Shaping

Bind off 4 (8) stitches at the beginning of the next 2 rows—65 (75) stitches.

Decrease 1 stitch at the beginning of the next 6 rows—59 (69) stitches.

Work 2 rows even.

Decrease 1 stitch at the beginning of the next 38 rows—21 (31) stitches.

Bind off 2 stitches at the beginning of the next 4 rows, then 3 stitches at the beginning of the next 2 (4) rows—7 (11) stitches.

Bind off the remaining stitches.

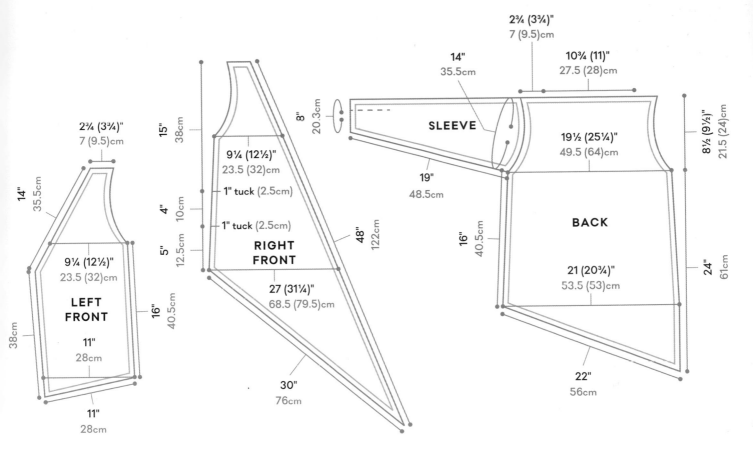

LEFT FRONT

2¾ (3¾)"
7 (9.5)cm

14"
35.5cm

9¼ (12½)"
23.5 (32)cm

38cm

16"
40.5cm

11"
28cm

11"
28cm

RIGHT FRONT

15"
38cm

4"
10cm

5"
12.5cm

9¼ (12½)"
23.5 (32)cm

1" tuck (2.5cm)

1" tuck (2.5cm)

8"
20.3cm

48"
122cm

27 (31¼)"
68.5 (79.5)cm

30"
76cm

SLEEVE

14"
35.5cm

19"
48.5cm

2¾ (3¾)"
7 (9.5)cm

BACK

10¾ (11)"
27.5 (28)cm

8½ (9½)"
21.5 (24)cm

19½ (25¼)"
49.5 (64)cm

16"
40.5cm

21 (20¾)"
53.5 (53)cm

24"
61cm

22"
56cm

FINISHING

BOTTOM EDGINGS

Back

With the RS facing, pick up and k105 (134) stitches. Knit 3 rows. Bind off knitwise on the RS.

Right Front

With the RS facing, pick up and k144 (174) stitches. Knit 3 rows. Bind off knitwise on the RS.

Left Front

With the RS facing, pick up and k56 (75) stitches. Knit 3 rows. Bind off knitwise on the RS.

Sew both shoulder seams.

Buttonhole Band

With the RS facing, pick up and k200 (214) stitches, starting at the bottom edge of the Right Front and ending at the shoulder seam.

Row 1 (WS): Knit.

Row 2: K7, *bind off 2 stitches, k16 (17); repeat from * 8 more times, knit to the end.

Row 3: Knit, casting on 2 stitches over each bind off on the previous row.

Bind off.

Button Band

With the RS facing, pick up and k111 (119) stitches, starting at the shoulder seam of the Left Front and ending at the bottom edge. Knit 3 rows. Bind off.

Neck Band

With the RS facing, pick up and k55 (54) stitches, starting at the right shoulder seam and ending at the left shoulder seam.

Knit 3 rows. Bind off. Sew side edges to Right and Left Front bands.

Set in the Sleeves. Sew left side and sleeve seams.

Following the schematic, measure and make two tucks on the Right Front side edge.

Sew right side and sleeve seams. Measure 7" (18cm) from the bottom and top center of the sleeve, and mark with a pin. Sew 9 buttons to the Left Front following the schematic, evenly spaced (approximately 2¼" [5.5cm] apart). With a threaded tapestry needle, work a running stitch to the pin, gather, and secure the yarn. Sew a button to the bottom to gather. Repeat for second sleeve.

chapter 2

COOL
CONSTRUCTION

This chapter showcases a variety of
nontraditional knit garments with creatively
constructed shapes and interesting details.
They are all inspiring and exciting to make,
whether you are combining a cleverly
placed scarf and a snap to create shaping,
constructing a jacket from two knitted circles
with sleeves extending from the center of
the circle, or working short rows and cabled
edgings at the same time for an avant garde
vest. This chapter is sure to spark some new
ideas and perhaps inspire you to explore
the possibilities of knitting without using the
traditional front, back, and two sleeves—just
for the thrill of it!

WEEKEND WARRIOR
wraparound

A bounty of colors is worked in short rows to create a large spellbinding circle. Instead of binding off the last row, the live stitches are threaded with a corresponding scarf, shaping the neck. A snap or two at the waist does the rest of the shaping for the tunic. To wear it as a cape just throw it around your shoulders and go. You can also bind off the last row and weave a scarf through the neckband instead of leaving the front stitches live. And yes, Weekend Warrior can easily be made in one weekend.

reimagine it
Live stitches and a scarf are used here to shape the neckline, but if you bind off those stitches, the cast-on and bound-off edges can become the front opening of a fun poncholette. Color combinations and multicolor yarn offer endless possibilities. An I-cord or even a thin belt could replace the scarf or ribbon.

SKILL LEVEL

TIME

SIZES

S (M, L), *shown in size S*

FINISHED MEASUREMENTS

Inner edge: 18½ (27¾, 37)" [47 (70.5, 94)cm]

Outer edge: 112 (130½, 149¼)" [284.5 (331.5, 379)cm]

Width: 16 (17½, 18¾)" [40.5 (44.5, 47.5)cm]

Note: The Body is made in one circular piece using short rows.

GAUGE

9 stitches and 18 rows = 4" (10cm) in garter stitch

Take time to check gauge.

MATERIALS

HPKY Flame (100% merino wool), 3½ oz (100g), 100 yd (91m); 1 ball of Grape (A), 1 ball of Lilac (B), 1 (2, 2) balls of Orchid (C), 1 ball of Blue (D), 1 ball of Teal (E), 1 ball of Green (F), 1 ball of Seafoam (G), 1 ball of Purple (H)

Size U.S. 15 (10mm) needles, or size needed to obtain gauge

2 size 10 snaps

Tapestry needle

Matching silk scarf (sample is shown with a hand-dyed scarf from HPKY) or ribbon

Circle Short Row Pattern

Row 1 (RS): K3, turn.
Row 2: Knit.
Row 3: Knit to the gap, k3, turn.
Row 4: Knit.
Rows 5–22 (5–24, 5–26): Repeat rows 3 and 4 until there are 3 stitches after the gap, end after a WS row.
Row 23 (25, 27): Knit.

SIZE S ONLY

Row 24: Purl.
Repeat rows 1–24 for pattern.

SIZE M ONLY

Row 26: Slip 1, p2, knit to the end.
Row 27: Knit.
Row 28: Purl.
Repeat rows 1–28 for pattern.

SIZE L ONLY

Rows 28 and 30: Slip 1, p2, knit to the end.
Rows 29 and 31: Knit.
Row 32: Purl.
Repeat rows 1–32 for pattern.

BODY

With A, cast on 36 (39, 42) stitches. Work 3 repeats of Circle Short Row pattern.

Work 2 repeats each of Circle Short Row pattern with B, C, D, and E.

With F, work 3 repeats of Circle Short Row pattern.

Work 2 repeats each of Circle Short Row pattern with G, H, and C.

With E, work 1 repeat of Circle Short Row pattern.

Do not bind off; cut yarn and secure.

FINISHING

Fold one end of the matching silk
scarf or ribbon, thread it through
the live stitches on the needle,
and gather it for the neckline.
Sew half the snap at the center of
the cast-on edge on the RS and
the other half at the center of the
G-to-H color-change row on the
WS. Sew 2nd snap where the
piece wraps at the waist line.
Tie scarf/ribbon at either the
neck, back, or the side.

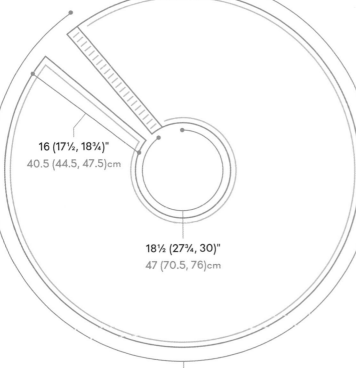

16 (17½, 18¾)"
40.5 (44.5, 47.5)cm

18½ (27¾, 30)"
47 (70.5, 76)cm

112 (130½, 149¼)"
284 (331.5, 379)cm

NOUVEAU
wrap cardigan

Make a grand entrance at the office, the theatre, a ball game, or any other event wearing this cardigan. Nouveau Wrap Cardigan is made with stockinette stitch and trimmed with an easy cable rib stitch. For drape and texture I chose a sensuous heathered alpaca yarn. Study the schematic to understand how the rectangles and curves come together for fit and at the same time include the scarves. One scarf end goes through a slit over the right shoulder and the other wraps over the left side and falls to the back.

reimagine it
I can see this design reworked in many ways using different colors and/or stitch patterns. Try using a two-color small repeat pattern, a check or a houndstooth pattern repeat for the stockinette stitch area, and then continue with a single color for the cable scarf and edging.

SKILL LEVEL

TIME

SIZES

S (M, L), *shown in size S*

FINISHED MEASUREMENTS

Back width: 18 (20, 22)" [45.5 (51, 56)cm]

Back length: 19½ (20½, 21½)" [49.5 (52, 54.5)cm]

GAUGE

21 stitches and 28 rows = 4" (10cm) in stockinette stitch

Take time to check gauge.

MATERIALS

Blue Sky Alpacas Melange (100% baby alpaca), 1¾ oz (50g), 110 yd (100m); 12 (14, 15) balls of #808 Olive

3 Size U.S. 6 (4mm) straight needles, or size needed to obtain gauge

Stitch holders

Removable stitch markers

Tapestry needle

Stitch Key

☐ K on RS, P on WS

⊡ P on RS, K on WS

⊠ RT

☐ Repeat

Baby Cable Rib

```
4 |·|·| | | |·|·|
                  3
2 |·|·|⊠| |·|·|
                  1
  6 5         1
```

Baby Cable Rib

RT: K2tog keeping both stitches on the left-hand needle, then knit the first stitch again, removing both stitches from the needle.

Row 1 (RS): P2, *k2, p2; repeat from * to the end.

Row 2: K2, *p2, k2; repeat from * to the end.

Row 3: P2, *RT, p2; repeat from * to the end.

Row 4: Repeat row 2.

Repeat rows 1–4 for pattern.

BACK

Cast on 94 (106, 116) stitches. Work in stockinette stitch for 18 (19, 20)" [45.5 (48.5, 51)cm], ending with a RS row.

Next row: P30 (34, 37) and place stitches on a holder for the left shoulder, bind off 34 (38, 42) stitches for the back neck, p30 (34, 37), and place stitches on a holder for the right shoulder.

Bottom Edging

With the RS facing, pick up and k94 (106, 116) stitches across the cast-on edge.

Setup row (WS): K2,*p2, k2; repeat from * to end.

Work 8 rows of Baby Cable Rib. Bind off in rib.

LEFT FRONT

Cast on 23 (26, 28) stitches.

Row 1 (WS): Purl.

Row 2: Knit to the end, cast on 2 stitches—25 (28, 30) stitches.

Repeat rows 1 and 2 two (three, four) more times—29 (34, 38) stitches.

Row 1: Purl.

Row 2 (RS): Knit to the last stitch, m1, k1—30 (35, 39) stitches.

Repeat Rows 1 and 2 35 (35, 37) more times—65 (70, 76) stitches.

Starting with a purl row, continue in stockinette stitch until piece

measures 18 (19, 20)" [45.5 (48.5, 51)cm] from the cast-on edge, ending with a WS row.
Next Row (RS): K30 (34, 37) and place these stitches on a holder for the shoulder, knit to the end.

Scarf
Continue in stockinette stitch on the remaining 35 (36, 39) stitches for 26" (66cm) more, ending with a WS row. Work 8 rows in Baby Cable Rib. Bind off in rib.

RIGHT FRONT
Cast on 23 (26, 28) stitches.
Row 1 (WS): Purl.
Row 2: Cast on 2 stitches, knit to end—25 (28, 30) stitches.
Repeat rows 1 and 2 two (three, four) more times—29 (34, 38) stitches.
Row 1: Purl.
Row 2 (RS): K1, m1, knit to the end—30 (35, 39) stitches.
Repeat Rows 1 and 2 35 (35, 37) more times—65 (70, 76) stitches.
Starting with a purl row, continue working in stockinette stitch until piece measures 14 (15, 16)" [35.5 (38, 40.5)cm] from the cast-on edge, ending with a WS row.

Scarf Slit
Next RS row: K54 (56, 59), place the last 22 stitches worked on a holder, knit to the end.
Next WS row: P11 (14, 17), cast on 22 stitches using the cable cast-on method (see page 169), p32 (34, 37).
Continue in stockinette stitch until piece measures 18 (19, 20)" [45.5 (48.5, 51)cm] from the bottom cast-on edge, ending with a RS row.

Next row (WS): P30 (34, 37) stitches and place them on a holder for the shoulder, knit to end.

Scarf
Continue in stockinette stitch on the remaining 35 (36, 39) stitches for 26" (66cm) more, ending with a WS row. Work 8 rows in Baby Cable Rib. Bind off in rib.

Slit Facing

With the RS facing, place the 22 stitches from the holder onto a noodle. Work 8 rows in Baby Cable Rib. Bind off in rib. Using the 3-needle bind-off method (see page 169), join shoulders. Mark 9 (9½, 10)" [23 (24, 25.5)cm] down from the shoulder seams on both Fronts and Back.

SLEEVES

With the RS facing, pick up and k94 (100, 106) stitches evenly spaced between markers on the Fronts and Back.
Starting with a purl row work 7 rows in stockinette stitch.
Decrease row (RS): K1, ssk, knit to the last 3 stitches, k2tog, k1.
Repeat Decrease row every 4th row 25 (24, 25) more times—42 (50, 54) stitches.
Work even in stockinette stitch until sleeve measures 16 (16½, 17)" [40.5 (42, 43)cm].
Work 12 rows in Baby Cable Rib. Bind off in rib.

FINISHING
Fronts and Neck Facing
With the RS facing, starting at the top shoulder side of the Right Front scarf, pick up and k116

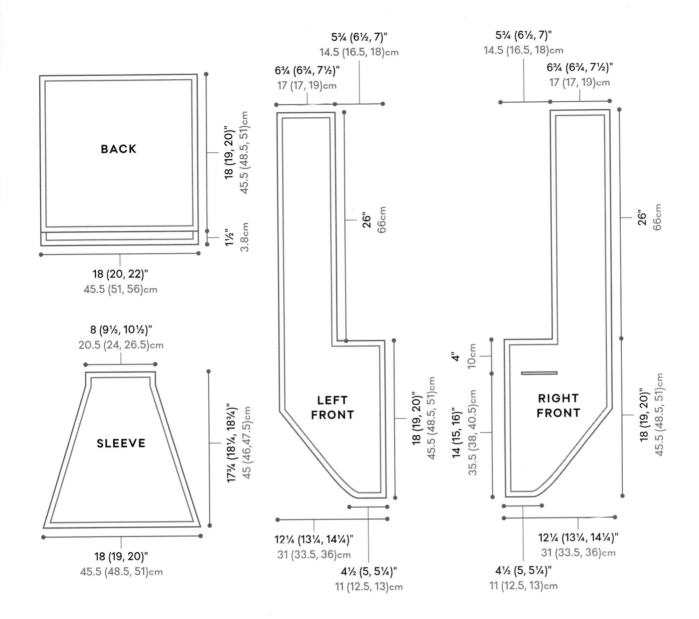

BACK

5¾ (6½, 7)"
14.5 (16.5, 18)cm

6¾ (6¾, 7½)"
17 (17, 19)cm

5¾ (6½, 7)"
14.5 (16.5, 18)cm

6¾ (6¾, 7½)"
17 (17, 19)cm

18 (19, 20)"
45.5 (48.5, 51)cm

1½"
3.8cm

18 (20, 22)"
45.5 (51, 56)cm

8 (9½, 10½)"
20.5 (24, 26.5)cm

SLEEVE

17¾ (18¼, 18¾)"
45 (46,47.5)cm

18 (19, 20)"
45.5 (48.5, 51)cm

26"
66cm

LEFT FRONT

18 (19, 20)"
45.5 (48.5, 51)cm

12¼ (13¼, 14¼)"
31 (33.5, 36)cm

4½ (5, 5¼)"
11 (12.5, 13)cm

26"
66cm

4"
10cm

RIGHT FRONT

14 (15, 16)"
35.5 (38, 40.5)cm

18 (19, 20)"
45.5 (48.5, 51)cm

12¼ (13¼, 14¼)"
31 (33.5, 36)cm

4½ (5, 5¼)"
11 (12.5, 13)cm

stitches to the shoulder seam, k34 (38, 42) Back neck stitches, pick up and k116 stitches to the top of the shoulder side of the Left Front scarf—266 (270, 274) stitches.

Setup row (WS): K2, *p2, k2; repeat from * to end.
Work 10 rows of Baby Cable Rib. Bind off in rib.

Right Front and Scarf Side Edging

With the RS facing and starting at bottom side seam, pick up and k262 (266, 270) stitches evenly spaced to the top edge of the scarf.

Setup row (WS): K2, *p2, k2; repeat from * to end.
Work 10 rows of Baby Cable Rib. Bind off in rib.

Left Front and Scarf Side Edging

Starting at top edge of the scarf and ending at the bottom side seam, work the same as for the Right Front and Scarf Side Edging.

Sew side and sleeve seams.

ON THE EDGE
dress

Everything about this design is soft, sensual, and feminine. It is made in stockinette stitch using a lightweight wool blend metallic yarn. The main feature of this dress is the side and bottom edging. Simple rectangles are edged with a corresponding color in faux fur yarn and then spot sewn to the dress creating a very stylish and unique detail. The front and back are knit with increases and decreases designed to hug and flatter the body. The teardrop openings at the neck add another sexy detail but could be sewn closed instead.

reimagine it
Envision the edging done with a colorful floral duplicate stitch, intarsia pattern, or a Fair Isle repeat. An easier idea might be colorful bold stripes. For a more textural look, use seed stitch in place of stockinette stitch.

SIZES

S (M, L, XL), *shown in size S*

FINISHED MEASUREMENTS

Bust: 31¼ (35¼, 39, 43¾)"
[79.5 (89.5, 99, 111)cm]

Length: 31 (32, 32¾, 33½)"
[79 (81, 83, 85)cm]

GAUGE

19 stitches and 30 rows = 4"
(10cm) on smaller needles in
stockinette stitch with A

Take time to check gauge.

MATERIALS

Berroco Flicker (87% baby alpaca,
8% acrylic, 5% other fibers), 1¾ oz
(50g), 189 yd (173m); 10 (11, 12,
13) balls of #3317 Dark Taupe (A)

Berroco Marmot (100% nylon),
1¾ oz (50g), 93 yd (85m); 2 (3, 4,
5) balls of #3703 Moonstone (B)

Size U.S. 8 (5mm) straight needles
and 16" (40.5cm) circular needle

Size U.S. 7 (4.5mm) straight
needles, or size needed to obtain
gauge

Stitch holders

Tapestry needle

FRONT

With B and larger needles, cast
on 110 (124, 138, 152) stitches.
Knit 3 rows.

Change to A and smaller needles.
Work in stockinette stitch for 8"
(20.5cm), ending with a WS row.
Bind off 15 stitches at the
beginning of the next 2 rows.
Bind off 2 (2, 3, 3) stitches at the
beginning of the next 6 rows—68
(82, 90, 104) stitches.

Waist Shaping

Decrease 1 stitch at the
beginning of the next 8 (12,
12, 16) rows—60 (70, 78, 88)
stitches.

Work even in stockinette stitch
until piece measures 15" (38cm)
from the cast-on edge, ending
with a WS row.

Increase row (RS): K1, m1, knit to
the last 3 stitches, m1, k1.
Repeat Increase row every RS row
4 more times—70 (80, 88, 98)
stitches.

Continue even in stockinette
stitch until piece measures 18"
(45.5cm), ending with a WS row.

Raglan Shaping

Bind off 4 (5, 6, 7) stitches at the
beginning of the next 2 rows—62
(70, 76, 84) stitches.

Decrease row (RS): K2, ssk, knit
to the last 4 stitches, k2tog, k2.
Continuing in stockinette stitch,
repeat Decrease row every RS
row 3 (9, 11, 17) more times, then
every 4th row 12 (10, 10, 8) times.
Place the remaining 30 (30, 32,
32) stitches on a holder.

Lower Front Side Edging

With the RS facing, B, and larger
needles, pick up and k40 stitches
along one 8" (20.5cm) side edge
of the lower front. Knit 3 rows.

Bind off. Repeat on the other side.

Front Bottom Panel
With B and larger needles, cast on 110 (124, 138, 152) stitches. Knit 3 rows.
Change to A and smaller needles. Work in stockinette stitch for 5" (12.5cm), ending with a WS row.
Change to B and larger needles. Knit 3 rows. Bind off.
With the RS facing, B, and larger needles, pick up and k28 stitches along one side of the panel. Knit 3 rows. Bind off. Repeat on the other side.

BACK
With B and larger needles, cast on 120 (134, 150, 168) stitches. Knit 3 rows.
Change to A and smaller needles. Work in stockinette stitch for 8" (20.5cm), ending with a WS row. Bind off 15 stitches at the beginning of the next 2 rows, bind off 2 (2, 3, 3) stitches at the beginning of the next 6 rows, then decrease 1 stitch at the beginning of the next 0 (4, 2, 10) rows—78 (88, 100, 110) stitches. Work even in stockinette stitch until piece measures the same as the front to the armhole, ending with a WS row.

Raglan Shaping

Bind off 4 (5, 6, 7) stitches at the beginning of the next 2 rows—70 (78, 88, 90) stitches.

Decrease row (RS): K2, ssk, knit to the last 4 stitches, k2tog, k2. Continuing in stockinette stitch, repeat Decrease row every RS row 3 (9, 11, 17) more times, then every 4th row 12 (10, 10, 8). Place the remaining 38 (38, 44, 44) stitches on a holder.

Lower Back Side Edging

With the RS facing, B, and larger needles, pick up and k40 stitches along one 8" (20.5cm) side edge of the lower back. Knit 3 rows. Bind off. Repeat on the other side.

Back Bottom Panel

With B and larger needles, cast on 120 (134, 150, 168) stitches. Knit 3 rows.

Change to A and smaller needles. Work in stockinette stitch for 5" (12.5cm), ending with a WS row. Change to B and larger needles. Knit 3 rows. Bind off.

With the RS facing, B, and larger needles, pick up and k28 stitches along the side of the panel. Knit 3 rows. Bind off. Repeat on the other side.

SLEEVES (MAKE 2)

With B and larger needles, cast on 52 (56, 60, 62) stitches. Knit 3 rows.

Change to A and smaller needles. Work 6 (6, 2, 6) rows in stockinette stitch.

Increase row (RS): K1, m1, knit to the last stitch, m1, k1. Repeat Increase row every 8th (6th, 6th, 4th) row 6 (9, 10, 14) more times— 66 (76, 82, 92) stitches.

Raglan Shaping

Work raglan shaping same as the Front. Place the remaining 26 stitches on a holder.

SIDE PANELS (MAKE 2)

With B and larger needles, cast on 128 stitches. Knit 3 rows. Change to A and smaller needles. Work in stockinette stitch for 5" (12.5cm), ending with a WS row. Change to B and larger needles. Knit 3 rows. Bind off.

With the RS facing, B, and larger needles, pick up and k28 stitches along one side of the panel. Knit 3 rows. Bind off. Repeat on the other side.

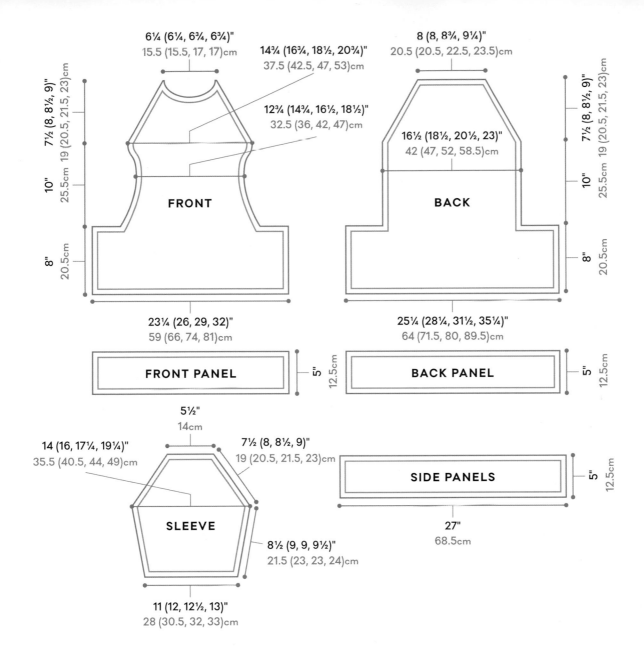

FRONT

6¼ (6¼, 6¾, 6¾)"
15.5 (15.5, 17, 17)cm

14¾ (16¾, 18½, 20¾)"
37.5 (42.5, 47, 53)cm

12¾ (14¾, 16½, 18½)"
32.5 (36, 42, 47)cm

7½ (8, 8½, 9)"
19 (20.5, 21.5, 23)cm

10"
25.5cm

8"
20.5cm

23¼ (26, 29, 32)"
59 (66, 74, 81)cm

BACK

8 (8, 8¾, 9¼)"
20.5 (20.5, 22.5, 23.5)cm

16½ (18½, 20½, 23)"
42 (47, 52, 58.5)cm

7½ (8, 8½, 9)"
19 (20.5, 21.5, 23)cm

10"
25.5cm

8"
20.5cm

25¼ (28¼, 31½, 35¼)"
64 (71.5, 80, 89.5)cm

FRONT PANEL

5"
12.5cm

BACK PANEL

5"
12.5cm

SLEEVE

5½"
14cm

14 (16, 17¼, 19¼)"
35.5 (40.5, 44, 49)cm

7½ (8, 8½, 9)"
19 (20.5, 21.5, 23)cm

8½ (9, 9, 9½)"
21.5 (23, 23, 24)cm

11 (12, 12½, 13)"
28 (30.5, 32, 33)cm

SIDE PANELS

5"
12.5cm

27"
68.5cm

FINISHING

The edgings may roll. Lightly steam flat.

Sew the Back raglan seams. Sew the Front raglan seams, leaving a 3½" (9cm) opening 1" (2.5cm) down from the top edge. Sew sleeve and side seams, leaving the lower front and back side edges open.

Neck Band

Starting at the Back right neck seam, place all stitches from the holders onto the circular needle—120 (120, 128, 128) stitches. With B, knit 3 rows. Bind off.

Assembly

With B, sew the Front and Back Bottom Panels for 1" (2.5cm) at

6 points evenly spaced across the lower edges of the dress, starting and ending at the side edges. With B, sew the Side Panels to the lower Front and Back side edges of the body for 1" (2.5cm) at 5 points evenly spaced across, starting and ending at the cast-on edges of the body and leaving the ends over the bottom panels free.

GLORY RISING CIRCLE
cardigan

This design consists of two large circles knitted from the outer edge to the center stitches, which are then used to continue knitting the ribbed sleeve. You heard me correctly: The circle extends into the sleeve! A variety of intriguing stitches and some easy color work are used to create the circle itself, which is shaped by strategic placement of decreases in between the stitches and row counts. The two circles are overlapped and sewn at the back, while the front collar is shaped by folding the outer edge back.

reimagine it
This could be created using two strong contrasting colors like black and white. And why not try making three quarter sleeves instead? You could even reimagine this piece using different circles or experimenting with other closures. It might be tricky, but it could be worth the effort.

TIME

SIZES

S (M, L/XL), *shown in size M*

FINISHED MEASUREMENTS

Bust: 36 (40, 50)" [91.5 (101.5, 127)cm]

Length: 22 (26, 29¼)" [56 (66, 74.5)cm]

Sleeve length: 15 (16, 17)" [38 (40.5, 43)cm]

GAUGE

16 stitches and 22 rows = 4" (10cm) in stockinette stitch

Take time to check gauge.

MATERIALS

Skacel Schulana Accordion (80% merino wool, 20% super-kid mohair), 1¾ oz (50g), 93 yd (85m): 10 (13, 15) balls of #13 Blue (A); 1 ball of #00 Natural (B); 1 ball of #09 Navy (C); 1 ball of #02 Orchid (D)

Size U.S. 9 (5.5mm) 24" (60cm), 32" (80cm), 40" (100cm), and 47" (120cm) circular needles as needed, and a set of 5 double-pointed needles, or size needed to obtain gauge

Stitch markers

Cable needle

Tapestry needle

3 toggle buckles

being careful not to twist the cast-on stitches.

Work 16 (24, 26) rnds of ribbing as follows:

*K2, p2; repeat from * around.

Decrease rnd 1: K1 (2, 2), k2tog, *[k1, k2tog] 3 (4, 3) times, k2, k2tog; repeat from * around—191 (226, 255) stitches.

Work 12 (16, 22) rnds of garter stitch as follows:

Purl 1 rnd, knit 1 rnd.

Decrease rnd 2:

Size S only: *P2tog, p3; repeat from * to the last 6 stitches, p2tog, p4—153 stitches.

Size M only: [P2tog, p3] twice, *p2tog, p2, [p2tog, p3] 10 times; repeat from * around—180 stitches.

Size L only: *P2tog, p3; repeat from * around—204 stitches.

Work 7 (9, 15) rnds in Cable Rib as follows, ending with rnd 1:

Rnd 1: *K2, p1; repeat from * around.

Rnd 2: *1/1 RC, p1; repeat from * around.

Decrease rnd 3:

Size S only: P2tog, p3, [p2tog, p2] twice, *[p2tog, p3] twice, p2tog, p2; repeat from * around—120 stitches.

Size M only: *P2tog, p3, p2tog, p2; repeat from * around—140 stitches.

Size L only: *P2tog, p2, ([p2tog,

Color Key

- ■ C
- □ B
- ■ D
- □ Repeat

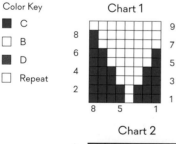

Chart 1 / Chart 2

Pattern Stitches

1/1 RC: Slip 1 stitch to cn and hold in back, k1, k1 from cn.

MB (make bobble): [K1, p1] twice, k1 all in the same stitch. Turn, k5; turn, pass the 2nd, 3rd, 4th, and 5th stitches over the first stitch.

CIRCLE (MAKE 2)

With longest circular needle and A, cast on 276 (328, 368) stitches loosely. Place marker and join for working in the round,

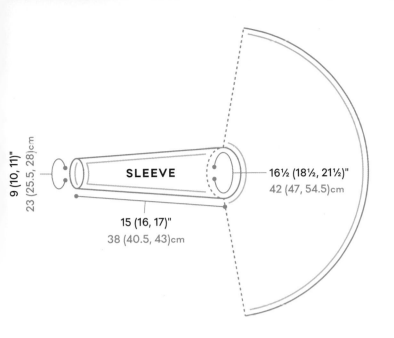

SLEEVE

9 (10, 11)" 23 (25.5, 28)cm

15 (16, 17)" 38 (40.5, 43)cm

16½ (18½, 21½)" 42 (47, 54.5)cm

12¼ (14½, 16¼)" 31 (37, 41)cm

22 (26, 29¼)" 56 (66, 74.5)cm

p3] twice, p2tog, p2) 7 times; repeat from * around—160 stitches.

Knit 2 rnds.

Next rnd: *K2, MB, k2; repeat from * around.

Knit 2 rnds.

Decrease rnd 4: *P2tog, p3; repeat from * around—96 (112, 128) stitches.

Change to B.

Next rnd: With B, knit.

Work 9 rnds of Chart 1.

Decrease rnd 5: With B, *[k2tog, k1] 4 times, k2tog, k2; repeat from * around—66 (77, 88) stitches.

Work 6 rnds of Chart 2.

SLEEVE

Change to A.

Rnd 1: With A, knit, decreasing 0 (3, 2) stitches evenly around—66 (74, 86) stitches.

Rnds 2–4: K2, *p2, k2; repeat from * around.

Decrease rnd: K2tog, work in rib to the last 2 stitches, ssk—2 stitches decreased.

Continuing in pattern as established, repeat Decrease rnd every 4th rnd 14 (16, 18) more times—36 (40, 48) stitches. Work even in rib until sleeve measures 15 (16, 17)" [38 (40.5, 43)cm] or to desired length. Bind off all stitches loosely in rib.

FINISHING

Place the circles side by side with the beginning of rounds together. Overlap one circle's ribbing on top of the other by 10 (12, 14)" [25.5 (30.5, 35.5)cm], measured along the beginning of the garter stitch section with the beginning of the rounds at the center. Pin in place, allowing the ribbing overlap to curve outward. Sew both right side and wrong side in place using a whipstitch (page 171). Fold the ribbed sections to the outside along the front edges and the top of the neck to form a shawl collar. Sew 3 toggle closures to the Front (see photograph for placement).

DIRECTIONAL
vest

Although easy to knit, the avant-garde construction will interest any knitter who likes the challenge of unusual shaping (take a quick look at the diagram). This design is shaped by using short rows and at the same time knitting the cabled edging around the front, back, and armholes. A cabled back insert pulls it all together, and cord closures embellish the front. Once you have made one of these vests, you will want to make it again and again.

reimagine it
I can see this vest reworked using a hand-painted yarn, but be careful the yarn isn't so busy that you lose the short-row and cabled edging patterns. Also try this with a clasp instead of the I-cord closure. Adding sleeves is another option.

TIME

SIZE

One size

FINISHED MEASUREMENTS

Back width (at underarm): 18" (45.5cm)

Back length: 21" (53.5cm)

GAUGE

14 stitches and 22 rows = 4" (10cm) in stockinette stitch

MATERIALS

Madelinetosh Tosh Chunky (100% superwash merino wool), 3½ oz (100g), 165 yd (151m); 4 skeins in Oceana

Size U.S. 10 (6mm) straight needles

Size U.S. 9 (5.5mm) set of 2 double-pointed needles

Cable needle

Stitch markers

Tapestry needle

Cable Rib
(multiple of 9 stitches + 5)

Row 1 (RS): *[P1, k1] twice, p1, k4; repeat from * to the last 5 stitches, p1, [k1, p1] twice.

Row 2: *[K1, p1] twice, k1, p4; repeat from * to the last 5 stitches, k1, [p1, k1] twice.

Row 3: *[P1, k1] twice, p1, 2/2 RC; repeat from * to the last 5 stitches, p1, [k1, p1] twice.

Row 4: Repeat row 2.

Repeat rows 1–4 for pattern.

CENTER BACK INSERT

Cast on 32 stitches.

Rows 1–28: Work 7 repeats of Cable Rib pattern.

Row 29 (RS): P1, ssk, work in pattern to the last 3 stitches, k2tog, p1—30 stitches.

Row 30: K1, p2tog, work in pattern to the last 3 stitches, p2tog tbl, k1—28 stitches.

Rows 31–42: Repeat rows 29 and 30—4 stitches after row 42.

Row 43: P1, k2tog, p1—3 stitches.

Row 44: S2kp—1 stitch.

Fasten off.

Right Armband

Cast on 14 stitches.

Work 60 rows in Cable Rib (15 cables), ending with row 4.

Note: From this point on, "Cable Rib" refers to working these 14 stitches as established.

Stitch Key

☐ K on RS, P on WS

⊡ P on RS, K on WS

▱ 2/2 RC

☐ Repeat

Cable Rib Pattern

Pattern Stitches

M2kp: Insert the left-hand needle, from front to back, under the horizontal bar between the last stitch worked and next stitch, k1 in the back loop, p1 in the back loop—2 stitches increased.

M2: Insert the left-hand needle from front to back under the horizontal bar between the last stitch worked and next stitch, k1 in the back loop, k1 in the front loop—2 stitches increased.

Pkp: [P1, k1, p1] into the same stitch—2 stitches increased.

2/2 RC: Slip 2 to cn and hold in back, k2, k2 from cn.

Increase row (RS): P1, [k1, p1] twice, k4, [p1, k1] twice, pkp—16 stitches.

Next row: K1, p1, Cable Rib. Continue in pattern as established until 28 rows (7 more cables) have been completed, ending with row 4.

RIGHT FRONT

Row 1 (RS): Work 13 stitches of Cable Rib, m2kp, p1, k1, p1—18 stitches.

Row 2: [K1, p1] twice, place marker, Cable Rib.

Row 3: Cable Rib, slip marker, m2kp, [k1, p1] twice—20 stitches.

Row 4: [K1, p1] 3 times, slip marker, Cable Rib.

Row 5: Cable Rib, slip marker, m2kp, [k1, p1] 3 times—22 stitches.

Row 6: K1, [p1, k1] twice, p3, slip marker, Cable Rib.

Row 7: Cable Rib, slip marker, m2kp, k3, p1, [k1, p1] twice—24 stitches.

Row 8: K1, [p1, k1] twice, p4, k1, slip marker, Cable Rib.

Row 9: Cable Rib, slip marker, m2kp, p1, k4, p1, [k1, p1] twice—26 stitches.

Row 10: K1, [p1, k1] twice, p4, k1, p1, k1, slip marker, Cable Rib.

Row 11: Cable Rib, slip marker, m2kp, k1, p1, 2/2 RC, p1, [k1, p1] twice—28 stitches.

Row 12: K1, [p1, k1] twice, p4, k1, [p1, k1] twice, slip marker, Cable Rib.

Row 13: Cable Rib, slip marker, m1, place marker, Cable Rib—29 stitches.

Row 14: Cable Rib, slip marker, p1, slip marker, Cable Rib.

Row 15: Cable Rib, slip marker, m2, knit to marker, slip marker, Cable Rib—31 stitches.

Rows 16 and 18: Cable Rib, slip marker, purl to marker, slip marker, Cable Rib.

Row 17: Cable Rib, slip marker, m1, knit to marker, slip marker, Cable Rib—32 stitches.

Rows 19–25: Repeat rows 15–18 twice, then rows 15–17 once more—38 stitches; 10 stitches between markers.

Note: From this point until row 291, stitch counts will not include Cable Ribs.

Row 26: Cable Rib, slip marker, p3, w&t.

Row 27: K3, slip marker, Cable Rib.

Row 28: Cable Rib, slip marker, purl to marker, slip marker, Cable Rib.

Rows 29–34: Repeat rows 15–17 once, then rows 26–28—13 stitches.

Rows 35–46: Repeat rows 29–34 twice—19 stitches.

Row 47: Cable Rib, slip marker, m2, k3, p16, slip marker, Cable Rib—21 stitches.

Row 48: Cable Rib, slip marker, k16, p5, slip marker, Cable Rib.

Rows 49 and 50: Repeat rows 17 and 18—22 stitches.

Rows 51–56: Repeat rows 29–34—25 stitches.

Row 57: Cable Rib, pbf, slip marker, knit to marker, slip marker, Cable Rib—26 stitches.

Row 58: Cable Rib, slip marker, purl to marker, slip marker, Cable Rib.

Row 59: Bind off 14 stitches, place marker, m2, knit to marker, slip marker, Cable Rib—28 stitches.

Row 60: Cable Rib, slip marker, purl to marker, slip marker, k1.

Row 61: P1, slip marker, m1, knit to marker, slip marker, Cable Rib—29 stitches.

Row 62: Cable Rib, slip marker, p3, w&t.

Row 63: K3, slip marker, Cable Rib.

Row 64: Cable Rib, slip marker, purl to marker, slip marker, k1.

Row 65: P1, slip marker, m2, knit to marker, slip marker, Cable Rib—31 stitches.

Rows 66–70: Repeat rows 60–64—32 stitches.

Row 71: P1, slip marker, m2, k3, purl to marker, slip marker, Cable Rib—34 stitches.

Row 72: Cable Rib, slip marker, knit to 5 stitches before marker, p5, slip marker, k1.

Row 73: P1, slip marker, m1, knit to marker, slip marker, Cable Rib—35 stitches.

Row 74: Cable Rib, slip marker, p3, w&t.

Row 75: K3, slip marker, Cable Rib.

Row 76: Cable Rib, slip marker, purl to marker, slip marker, k1.

Row 77: P1, slip marker, m2, knit to marker, slip marker, Cable Rib—37 stitches.

Row 78: Cable Rib, slip marker, p17, w&t.

Row 79: Knit to marker, slip marker, Cable Rib.

Row 80: Cable Rib, slip marker, purl to marker, slip marker, k1.

Rows 81–96: Repeat rows 73–80 twice—43 stitches.

Rows 97–122: Repeat rows 71–96—54 stitches.

Row 123: Purl to the 2nd marker, slip marker, Cable Rib.

Row 124: Cable Rib, slip marker, knit to end.

Row 125: P1, slip marker, k1, ssk, knit to marker, slip marker, Cable Rib—53 stitches.

Row 126: Cable Rib, slip marker, p3, w&t.

Row 127: K3, slip marker, Cable Rib.

Row 128: Cable Rib, slip marker, purl to 3 stitches before the next marker, p2tog tbl, p1, slip marker, k1—52 stitches.

Row 129: Repeat row 125—51 stitches.

Row 130: Cable Rib, slip marker, p17, w&t.

Row 131: K17, slip marker, Cable Rib.

Row 132: Repeat row 128—50 stitches.

Rows 133–148: Repeat rows 125–132 twice—42 stitches.

Rows 149–152: Repeat rows 125–128—40 stitches.

Rows 153 and 154: Repeat rows 123 and 124.

Row 155: P1, slip marker, k2, m1, knit to marker, slip marker, Cable Rib—41 stitches.

Row 156: Cable Rib, slip marker, p3, w&t.

Row 157: K3, slip marker, Cable Rib.

Row 158: Cable Rib, slip marker, purl to 2 stitches before the next marker, m1p, p2 slip marker, k1—42 stitches.

Row 159: Repeat row 155—43 stitches.

Row 160: Cable Rib, slip marker, p17, w&t.

Row 161: K17, slip marker, Cable Rib.

Row 162: Repeat row 158—44 stitches.

Rows 163–182: Repeat rows 155–162 twice, then rows 155–158 once—54 stitches.

Rows 183 and 184: Repeat rows 123 and 124.

Row 185: P1, slip marker, k3tog, knit to marker, slip marker, Cable Rib—52 stitches.

Row 186: Cable Rib, slip marker, p17, w&t.

Row 187: K17, slip marker, Cable Rib.

Row 188: Cable Rib, slip marker, purl to marker, slip marker, k1.

Row 189: P1, slip marker, k2tog, knit to marker, slip marker, Cable Rib—51 stitches.

Row 190: Cable Rib, slip marker, p3, w&t.

Row 191: K3, slip marker, Cable Rib.

Row 192: Cable Rib, slip marker, purl to marker, slip marker, k1.

Rows 193–208: Repeat rows 185–192 twice—45 stitches.

Row 209: P1, slip marker, k3tog, k2, purl to marker, slip marker, Cable Rib—43 stitches.

Row 210: Cable Rib, slip marker, knit to 3 stitches before the next marker, p3, slip marker, k1.

Rows 211–236: Repeat rows 185–210—32 stitches.

Row 237: P1, slip marker, k3tog, knit to marker, slip marker, Cable Rib—30 stitches.

Row 238: Cable Rib, slip marker, p3, w&t.

Row 239: K3, slip marker, Cable Rib.

Row 240: Cable Rib, slip marker, purl to marker, slip marker, k1.

Row 241: P1, slip marker, k2tog, knit to marker, slip marker, Cable Rib—29 stitches.

Row 242: Cable Rib, slip marker, purl to marker, slip marker, k1.

Rows 243–246: Repeat rows 237–240—27 stitches.

Row 247: Cast on 14 stitches, Cable Rib 13 stitches, p2tog, place marker, knit to marker, slip marker, Cable Rib—54 stitches total, 26 stitches between markers.

Row 248: Cable Rib, slip marker, purl to marker, slip marker, Cable Rib.

Row 249: Cable Rib, slip marker, k3tog, knit to marker, slip marker, Cable Rib—24 stitches.

Row 250: Cable Rib, slip marker, p3, w&t.

Row 251: K3, slip marker, Cable Rib.

Row 252: Cable Rib, slip marker, purl to marker, slip marker, Cable Rib.

Row 253: Cable Rib, slip marker, k2tog, knit to marker, slip marker, Cable Rib—23 stitches.

Row 254: Cable Rib, slip marker, purl to marker, slip marker, Cable Rib.

Row 255: Cable Rib, slip marker, k3tog, knit to marker, slip marker, Cable Rib—21 stitches.

Row 256: Cable Rib, slip marker, p3, w&t.

Row 257: K3, slip marker, Cable Rib.

Row 258: Cable Rib, slip marker, purl to marker, slip marker, Cable Rib.

Row 259: Cable Rib, slip marker, k3tog, k2, p16, slip marker, Cable Rib—19 stitches.

Row 260: Cable Rib, slip marker, k16, p3, slip marker, Cable Rib.

Row 261: Cable Rib, k2tog, knit to marker, slip marker, Cable Rib—18 stitches.

Row 262: Cable Rib, slip marker, p3, w&t.

Row 263: K3, slip marker, Cable Rib.

Row 264: Cable Rib, slip marker, purl to marker, slip marker, Cable Rib.

Row 265: Cable Rib, slip marker, k3tog, knit to marker, slip marker, Cable Rib—16 stitches.

Row 266: Cable Rib, slip marker, purl to marker, slip marker, Cable Rib.

Rows 267–280: Repeat rows 261–266 twice—10 stitches.

Row 281–284: Repeat rows 263–266—8 stitches.

Row 285: Cable Rib, slip marker, k2tog, knit to marker, slip marker, Cable Rib—7 stitches.

Row 286: Cable Rib, slip marker,

purl to marker, slip marker, Cable Rib.

Row 287: Cable Rib, slip marker, k3tog, knit to marker, slip marker, Cable Rib—5 stitches.

Row 288: Repeat row 286.

Rows 289–290: Repeat rows 285–288—2 stitches.

Row 291: Cable Rib, slip marker, k2tog, slip marker, Cable Rib—29 stitches.

Row 292: Cable Rib, remove marker, p1, slip marker, Cable Rib.

LEFT FRONT

Row 293: Cable Rib, slip marker, k3tog, continue in pattern to end—27 stitches.

Row 294: Work in pattern to marker, slip marker, Cable Rib.

Rows 295–302: Repeat rows 293 and 294—19 stitches.

Row 303: Cable Rib, slip marker, k2tog, p1, k1, p1—18 stitches.

Row 304: K1, p3tog, Cable Rib—16 stitches.

Next row: Cable Rib, k1, p1. Continue in Cable Rib as established until 27 rows (7 more cables) have been completed, ending with row 3 of pattern.

Decrease row (WS): K3tog, work in pattern to end—14 stitches.

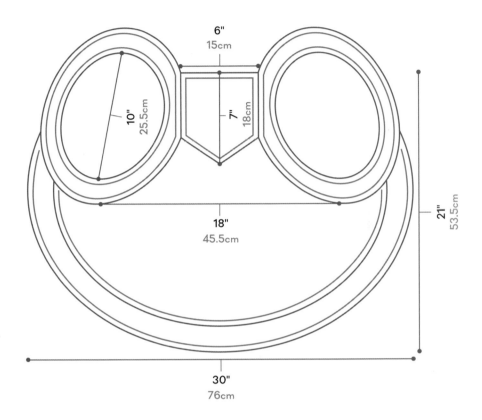

Left Armband

Work 60 rows in Cable Rib (15 cables).
Bind off in pattern.

FINISHING

Sew the cast-on ends to the bound-off ends of the armbands. Beginning at the center back point, sew the Center Back Insert to the center of the V. Sew the armbands to the back armholes and the sides of the insert, matching the small increases in each band to the top edge of the insert.

I-cord Closure (MAKE 2)

Cast on 3 stitches onto a double-pointed needle.

Row 1: Do not turn. Slide stitches to right end of needle, k3.
Repeat Row 1 for 24" (61cm). Bind off.
Starting at the center, form a spiral approximately 1½" (3.8cm) wide, leaving remaining 14" (35.5cm) for the tie, and sew to secure. Knot the ends of each cord.
Sew each closure to the Front (see photograph for placement).

SHAPE-SHIFTER
vest

The fusion of two slightly shaped rectangular pieces becomes a forward-looking, nontraditional vest. I will let you in on a designer secret: This vest started out as sleeves for a coat, but when I put the pieces on my mannequin they overlapped, and with a little twisting and stitching, became the Shape-Shifter Vest. The contrasting cord trim is sewn on and twisted to resemble the organic shape of a tree branch. Knitting accidents like this one can be wonderfully inventive.

reimagine it
Try this design using a different rib stitch for the overall pattern; just be careful of your gauge. Or try using a lovely multicolored hand-dyed yarn for a stylish look. It might also be interesting to use a textured bobble or cabled I-cord for the edging. See my book *Knitting over the Edge* for a variety of I-cord patterns.

TIME

SIZES

S/M (L/XL), *shown in size S/M*

FINISHED MEASUREMENTS

Bust: 40 (48)" [101.5 (122)cm]
Length: 27½ (28)" [70 (72.5)cm]

GAUGE

12 stitches and 16 rows = 4"
(10cm) in stockinette stitch on
larger needles

18 stitches and 10 rows = 4"
(10cm) in Eyelet Rib pattern on
larger needles

MATERIALS

Cascade 128 Superwash (100%
superwash merino wool), 3½ oz
(100g), 128 yd (117m); 7 (9)
skeins of #1926 Tan (MC), 1 skein
of #1981 Brown (CC)

Size U.S. 10½ (6.5mm) straight
needles, or size needed to obtain
gauge
Size U.S. 10 (6mm) double-
pointed needles
Stitch holders
Tapestry needle

Eyelet Rib Pattern
(multiple of 7 stitches + 3)
Row 1 (RS): P3, *k4, p3; repeat
from * to end.
Row 2: K1, yo, k2tog, *p4, k1, yo,
k2tog; repeat from * to end.
Repeat rows 1 and 2 for pattern.

LEFT/RIGHT SIDE
(MAKE 2)
With larger needles and MC,
cast on 52 (59) stitches.
Work in Eyelet Rib pattern for
18 (19)" [45.5 (48.5)cm], ending
with a WS row.

Note: Lengthen or shorten here
as desired.

Armhole Shaping
Bind off 7 (9) stitches at the
beginning of the next RS row,
then bind off 2 (3) stitches at
the beginning of the following RS
row—43 (47) stitches.
Continue in pattern as
established for 16" (40.5cm),
ending with a WS row.
Cast on 2 (3) stitches at the
beginning of the next RS row,
then cast on 7 (9) stitches at the
beginning of the following RS
row—52 (59) stitches.
Continue in pattern as
established for 18 (19)" [45.5
(48.5)cm]. Bind off.

FINISHING
Fold each piece in half widthwise
at the center of the armhole
and sew the side seam. Join the
two sides following the diagram,
adjusting for fit as necessary.

I-cord Trim
With dpns and B, cast on 5
stitches and work I-cords (see
page 170) to the lengths listed
below. When each cord is the
desired length, do not bind off;
place stitches on a holder.

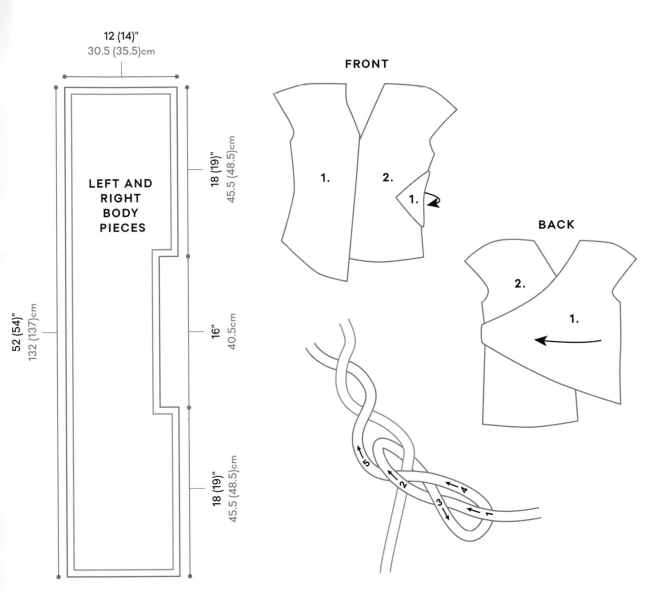

FRONT

1.   2.   1.

BACK

2.

1.

- 2 Armhole Cords, 18 (19)" [45.5 (48.5)cm] each

- 1 Body Cord, 96 (100)" [244 (254)cm]

- 1 Lower Left Front Cord, 6 (7)" [15 (18)cm]

Sew the Armhole Cords to armholes, beginning with the cast-on end at the underarm seam, lengthening or shortening the cord as needed.

Starting at the lower right front, sew the Body Cord to 13 (14)" [33 (35.5)cm] of the edge, leave the next 7" (18cm) of the cord and front edge unattached, continue sewing up the right front neck and down the right center back, leaving the last ½" (13mm) of cord and back edge unattached; sew the corner.

Following the diagram above, loop around the unattached sections and continue twisting

around the 7" (18cm) unattached section. Sew the twist section and continue to sew up the left front and left back neck. Adjust the length if necessary, bind off, and sew to the front.

Adjust the length of the Lower Left Front Cord if necessary, bind off, and sew to the lower left front edge.

chapter 3

WOVEN WEAVES

Some of my previous designs that have included weaving have proven so popular with knitters and seemed to have such an impact in our knitting world that I decided to devote an entire chapter to woven pieces. Although they may look complicated, you'll quickly discover that they are as simple to make as an easy braid or a child's loomed potholder. Color choices here also have a big impact; with hand-dyed variegated yarn, each piece is one of a kind, because you never know where the colors will end up in the finished garment.

CRISSCROSS WEAVE
tank

This peaceful design is so simple to knit even though it uses two weaving techniques, braiding and woven weaves. The shoulder straps are three braided cords, woven together and sewn in place at the back for a more exciting detail and fit. Squares sewn into the side seams add an unusual drape to the design, complementing the thick and thin cotton ribbon yarn used for a zen look. A perfect piece for hot weather or winter wear over another garment.

reimagine it
To make a more fitted piece, leave out the squares sewn into the sides and sew the whole side seam. I can see this tank made longer and becoming a sexy dress or even a gown, especially if you use a yarn with some bling in it.

TIME

SIZES

S (M, L), *shown in size S*

FINISHED MEASUREMENTS

Bust: 33 (38½, 44)" [84 (98, 112)cm]

Length: 25 (27, 29)" [63.5 (68.5, 74)cm]

GAUGE

20 stitches and 24 rows = 4" (10cm) in stockinette stitch

Take time to check gauge.

MATERIALS

Tahki Yarns Ripple (100% mercerized cotton), 1¾ oz (50g), 142 yd (130m); 5 (6, 8) balls of color #10 Pewter

Size U.S. 8 (5mm) straight needles, or size needed to obtain gauge

Spare needle for holding stitches

Stitch holders

6 large safety pins

Tapestry needle

POCKET LININGS

(MAKE 2)

Cast on 19 stitches. Work in stockinette stitch for 3½" (9cm). Leave on a spare needle.

FRONT

Cast on 100 (116, 132) stitches. Work 10 (8, 6) rows in stockinette stitch.

Decrease row (RS): K1, k2tog, knit to the last 3 stitches, ssk, k1. Repeat Decrease row every 10th row 8, (9, 10) more times—82 (96, 110) stitches.

At the same time, when piece measures 5½" (14cm) from the cast-on edge, make the first pocket as follows:

Next Row (RS): Knit to the last 30 stitches and place the next 19 stitches onto a holder; knit the 19 held stitches of Pocket Lining 1, knit to the end. Continue in stockinette stitch and decrease as established until piece measures 9" (23cm) from the cast-on edge for the second pocket.

Next Row (RS): K10, place the next 19 stitches onto a holder, knit the 19 held stitches of Pocket Lining 2, knit to the end. Continue as established until piece measures 16 (17, 18)" [40.5 (43, 45.5)cm], ending with a WS row.

Shape Armholes

Bind off 5 (7, 8) stitches at the beginning of the next 2 rows—72 (82, 94) stitches.

Decrease row (RS): K1, k2tog, knit to the last 3 stitches, ssk, k1. Repeat Decrease row every RS row 3 (4, 6) more times—64 (72, 80) stitches.

Work even in stockinette stitch until armhole measures 5 (5½, 6)" [12.5 (14, 15)cm], ending with a WS row.

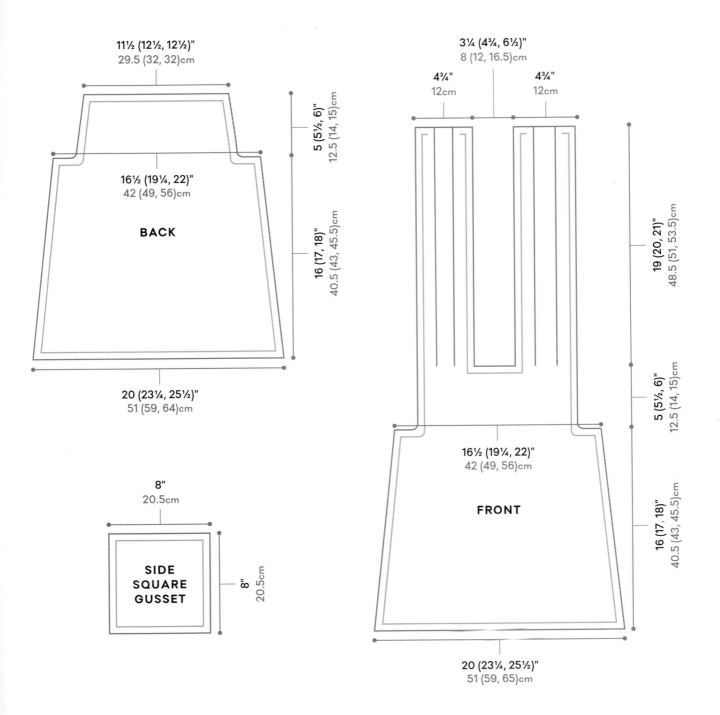

11½ (12½, 12½)"
29.5 (32, 32)cm

5 (5½, 6)"
12.5 (14, 15)cm

16½ (19¼, 22)"
42 (49, 56)cm

BACK

16 (17, 18)"
40.5 (43, 45.5)cm

20 (23¼, 25½)"
51 (59, 64)cm

3¼ (4¾, 6½)"
8 (12, 16.5)cm

4¾"
12cm

4¾"
12cm

19 (20, 21)"
48.5 (51, 53.5)cm

5 (5½, 6)"
12.5 (14, 15)cm

16½ (19¼, 22)"
42 (49, 56)cm

FRONT

16 (17, 18)"
40.5 (43, 45.5)cm

20 (23¼, 25½)"
51 (59, 65)cm

8"
20.5cm

**SIDE
SQUARE
GUSSET**

8"
20.5cm

Neck Shaping and Crisscross Strips

Next Row (RS): K24 and place these stitches on a holder, bind off the next 16 (24, 32) stitches, [k8 and place these stitches on a safety pin] twice, k8.

Work in stockinette stitch on these 8 stitches for 19 (20, 21)" [48.5 (51, 53.5)cm] and place stitches on a safety pin.

Slip the next set of 8 stitches onto a needle and work in stockinette stitch for 19 (20, 21)" [48.5 (51, 53.5)cm]. Repeat for the remaining set of 8 stitches. Repeat for the opposite set of 24 stitches.

BACK

Work same as the Front to the neck shaping, omitting the pockets—64 (72, 80) stitches. Decrease 6 (9, 17) stitches evenly across the next row, leaving the remaining 58 (63, 63) stitches on a spare needle.

SIDE SQUARE GUSSETS
(MAKE 2)

Cast on 40 stitches and work in stockinette stitch for 8" (20.5cm). Bind off.

FINISHING

Make 6" (15cm) braids at the front ends of the strips and stitch to secure them, then crisscross the strips following the photo (right), adjusting length if necessary. Place the 6 strips onto a needle and join, evenly spaced, to the 58 (63, 63) Back stitches, using the 3-needle bind-off (see page 169) as follows:
[Bind off 8 strip stitches together with 8 Back stitches, bind off 2 (3, 3) Back stitches only] 5 times, bind off 8 strip stitches together with 8 Back stitches.

Starting at the underarm, sew the side seam, leaving 8" (20.5cm) up from the bottom open. Insert the Side Square Gusset and sew two consecutive sides, as a triangle, into the opening. Repeat for the other side seam.

With the RS facing, place the front pocket stitches onto a needle. Bind off the stitches and using a long tail, sew the edges of the pocket linings to the inside of the garment.

Press seams lightly.

BRAIDED VITALITY
pullover

Featuring a bold all-over rib pattern, this pullover is worked in three pieces: a front, a back, and a combined bodice and sleeves made in one piece. The dramatic design is all about the center braid on the front of the sweater. The sleeves and shoulders have been knitted cuff to cuff and are sewn to the front and back pieces. The rectangular neck band is knit separately and sewn on, bringing this revolutionary pullover together in a medley of lovely color striping.

reimagine it
This was such a fun, quick piece to make. I used Lion Brand's Da Vinci yarn, which comes in many great colors you can choose from for this piece. Imagine this pullover made longer into a tunic or dress. You could wear it with fun leggings or tights and a cool pair of boots!

SKILL LEVEL

TIME

SIZES

S/M (L/XL), *shown in size S/M*

FINISHED MEASUREMENTS

Bust: 43 (48)" [109 (122)cm]

Length: 23¼ (25¼)" [59 (64)cm]

Sleeve length to underarm: 16 (17)" [40.5 (43)cm]

GAUGE

13 stitches and 17 rows = 4" (10cm) in k2, p2 rib

Take time to check gauge.

MATERIALS

Lion Brand Da Vinci (53% wool, 47% acrylic), 1¾ oz (50g), 55 yd (50m); 14 (16) skeins of #207 Quartz

SUPER BULKY

Size U.S. 10½ (6.5mm) straight needles, or size needed to obtain gauge

Stitch markers

Waste yarn or stitch holders

Matching worsted-weight yarn for seaming

Tapestry needle

K2, P2 Rib

(multiple of 4 stitches + 2)

Row 1 (RS): *P2, k2; rep from * to last 2 stitches, p2.

Row 2: *K2, p2; repeat from * to last 2 stitches, k2.

Repeat rows 1 and 2 for pattern.

FRONT

Cast on 70 (78) stitches.

Work 6 rows in k2, p2 Rib pattern.

Setup row (RS): Work 17 (21) stitches in rib, place marker, work [12 stitches in rib, place marker] 3 times, work 17 (21) stitches in rib.

Working on the last set of 17 (21) stitches only, work in rib as established for 17" (43cm), ending with WS row. Place stitches on a holder.

*Join new yarn to the next set of 12 stitches ready to work a WS row, and work in rib as established for 20" (51cm), ending with WS row. Place these stitches on a holder; repeat from * for the next 2 sets of 12 stitches.

Join new yarn to the last set of 17 (21) stitches ready to work a WS row, and work in rib as established for 17" (43cm), ending with a WS row.

Following the photograph, braid the three center strips tightly. Place all 70 (78) stitches back onto the same needle ready to work a RS row.

Work 4 rows in rib as established. Bind off in pattern.

BACK

Cast on 70 (78) stitches. Work in rib pattern until piece measures 17" (43cm). Bind off.

RIGHT SLEEVE

Cast on 34 (38) stitches. Work in rib pattern for 8" (20.5cm).

Increase row (RS): Work 1 stitch in rib, m1p, work in rib to the last

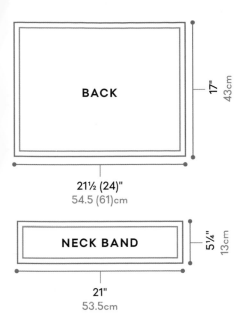

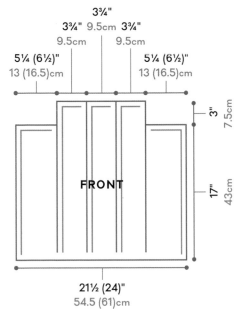

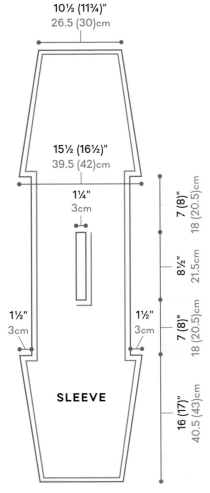

stitch, m1p, work 1 stitch in rib. Repeat Increase row every 4th row 7 more times, working increased stitches into pattern and using either m1 or m1p as needed—50 (54) stitches. Work even in rib as established until piece measures 16 (17)" [40.5 (43)cm] or desired length to underarm, ending with a WS row.

Bind off 5 stitches at the beginning of the next 2 rows—40 (44) stitches.

Yoke
Work even in rib for 7 (8)" [18 (20.5)cm], ending with a WS row.

Neck Shaping
Next row (RS): Work 18 (20) stitches in rib, join new yarn and bind off the next 4 stitches, work 18 (20) stitches in rib. Work both sides at the same time in rib as established for 8½" (21.5cm), ending with a WS row.
Next row (RS): Using one yarn across all stitches, work 18 (20) stitches in rib, cast on 4 stitches,

work 18 (20) stitches in rib—40 (44) stitches.
Continue in rib as established for 7 (8)" [18 (20.5cm], ending with a WS row.

LEFT SLEEVE
Continuing in rib, cast on 5 stitches at the beginning of the next 2 rows—50 (54) stitches. Work 4 rows even in rib.
Decrease row (RS): Work 1 stitch in rib, p2tog, work in rib to the last 3 stitches, p2tog, work 1 stitch in rib.
Repeat Decrease row every 4th row 7 more times, using either k2tog or p2tog as needed—34 (38) stitches.
Work even in rib until left sleeve measures 16 (17)" [40.5 (43)cm] from underarm.
Bind off.

FINISHING
Note: Use a plain worsted-weight yarn for sewing.
Sew Front and Back side seams.

Sew sleeve seams. Pin yoke to Front and Back, matching side and underarm stitches, and sew in place, easing yoke stitches across the Front and Back.

Neck Band
Cast on 17 stitches.
Row 1 (RS): *K2, p2; repeat from * to the last stitch, k1. Work in pattern as established for 21" (53.5cm). Bind off. Sew cast-on edge to bound-off edge. Using the k1 edge as the seam stitch, sew Neck Band to the neck opening, centering the seam at center back.

ETIQUETTE UNCHAINED
pullover

You are sure to be in the spotlight when you wear this colorful woven pullover. This piece is reminiscent of other designs I've created over the years but with several twists. It is knit from the top down using stockinette stitch strips in a multicolor yarn, which assures each of these will look like a true original. Whether you are a novice or an advanced knitter, I think you will enjoy the excitement of making this piece. The woven strips require some extra fussing and sewing but it is worth it.

reimagine it
Envision this pullover as a vest: Simply leave off the sleeves. Using the Mochi Plus multicolor skeins also ensures your piece will look different than mine. Every project becomes one of a kind. This technique is also lovely in solid colors. Try belting the finished garment.

SKILL LEVEL

TIME

SIZES

S (M, L, XL), *shown in size M*

FINISHED MEASUREMENTS

Bust: 35 (37½, 41½, 48)" [89 (95, 105.5, 122)cm]

Length: 27 (28, 29, 30)" [68.5 (71, 74, 76)cm]

Note: Length is approximate. Garment is draped on the bias and is highly elastic. It is worked from the top down.

Sleeve length to underarm: 17½ (17½, 18, 18)" [44.5 (44.5, 45.5, 45.5)cm]

GAUGE

18 stitches and 22 rows = 4" (10cm) in stockinette stitch

Take time to check gauge.

MATERIALS

Crystal Palace Mochi Plus (80% wool, 20% nylon), 1¾ oz (50g), 95 yd (87m); 13 (14, 16, 18) balls of #608 Rainbow Trout

Size U.S. 10 (6mm) needles, or size needed to obtain gauge

Tapestry needle

FRONT (MAKE 2)

Note: Neck and strips have some natural roll.

Starting at the shoulder, cast on 28 (31, 34, 37) stitches. Purl 1 row.

Increase row (RS): *K1, m1; repeat from * to end—56 (62, 68, 74) stitches.

Work even in stockinette stitch until piece measures 7 (7, 7½, 8)" [18 (18, 19, 20.5)cm], ending with a WS row.

Strip 1

K19 (21, 23, 25), leaving the remaining stitches on the needle.

Increase row (WS): P1, m1, purl to the last stitch, m1, p1—21 (23, 25, 27) stitches.

Work even in stockinette stitch for 20 (21, 21½, 22)" [51 (53.5, 54.5, 56)cm], ending with a RS row.

Knit 4 rows. Bind off.

Strip 2

With the RS facing, join yarn to the next stitch and k18 (20, 22, 24).

Increase row (WS): P1, m1, purl to the last stitch, m1, p1—20 (22, 24, 26) stitches.

Continue as for Strip 1.

Strip 3

Work the same as Strip 1.

BACK

Make 2 pieces the same as the Front.

SLEEVES

Note: The sleeves are knit from the top down.

Cast on 64 (64, 68, 72) stitches. Work in stockinette stitch for 2" (5cm), ending with a WS row.

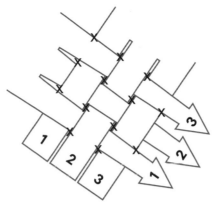

X = knotted stitch

Decrease row (RS): K1, k2tog, knit to the last 3 stitches, ssk, k1. Repeat Decrease row every 6th row 12 (12, 11, 9) times, then every 4th row 2 (2, 4, 7) times—34 (34, 36, 38) stitches. Work even in stockinette stitch until sleeve measures 17½ (17½, 18, 18)" [44.5 (44.5, 45.5, 45.5) cm], ending with a RS row. Knit 4 rows. Bind off.

FINISHING

Gently press strips, allowing the sides of each strip to roll slightly to the wrong side.
Weave the Fronts together following the diagram above.
Flip the piece over so the wrong side faces up. Tack the strips in place at each corner as pictured in the diagram.
Weave the Backs together the same as the Fronts.
Sew the shoulder seams. Sew in the Sleeves. Sew the side and sleeve seams.

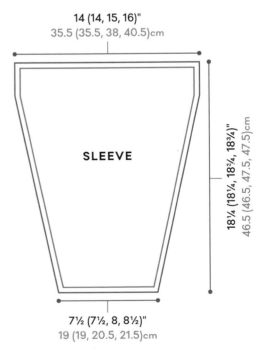

6¼ (7, 7½, 8¼)"
15.5 (18, 19, 21)cm

BACK AND FRONT

7 (7, 7½, 8)"
18 (18, 19, 20.5)cm

20¾ (21¼, 22¼, 23¾)"
53 (55.5, 56.5, 63)cm

4½"
11.5cm

4"
10cm

4½"
11.5cm

13¾ (15¼, 16½, 17¾)"
35 (38.5, 42, 45)cm

14 (14, 15, 16)"
35.5 (35.5, 38, 40.5)cm

SLEEVE

18¼ (18¼, 18¾, 18¾)"
46.5 (46.5, 47.5, 47.5)cm

7½ (7½, 8, 8½)"
19 (19, 20.5, 21.5)cm

PIXILATED WEAVE
drapelette

An interesting woven I-cord wakes up the casual drape of this go-anywhere design. It is knit from side to side using rib-stitch cuffs and a stockinette-stitch body with a series of decreases to shape the deep flattering angle. The knitted cord looks as though it is knitted into the background but it is actually woven, pinned, and sewn on after the piece is knit. Try a contrasting color for the cord if you like, substitute one of the many cord applications and motifs in my other books, or make up your own!

reimagine it
Even if you leave the background piece the same, there are hundreds of different ways you can embellish this sweater using knitted cords, flowers, leaves, bobbles, colorwork, or embroidery! Or try a multicolored yarn with complementary colors for the embellishments.

TIME

SIZE

One size

FINISHED MEASUREMENTS

Bust: 73½" (186.5cm)

Cuff to cuff: 36¾" (93.5cm)

Length: 13¾–25½" (35–65cm)

GAUGE

16 stitches and 22 rows = 4" (10cm) in stockinette stitch on larger needles

Take time to check gauge.

MATERIALS

Fyberspates Scrumptious Aran (45% silk, 55% merino), 3½ oz (100g), 180 yd (165m); 7 balls of #409 Teal Green

Size U.S. 9 (5.5mm) straight needles, or size needed to obtain gauge

Size U.S. 7 (4.5mm) straight needles and double-pointed needles

Stitch holders or large safety pins

Tapestry needle

FRONT

With larger needles, cast on 55 stitches.

Work 2 rows in stockinette stitch.

Increase row (RS): K1, m1, knit to the end.

Continuing in stockinette stitch, repeat Increase row every 4th row until there are 102 stitches. Work even for 2½" (6.5cm), until piece measures 34½" (87.5cm). Bind off.

BACK

Work same as Front, working Increase row as follows:

Increase row (RS): Knit to the last stitch, m1, k1.

FINISHING

Match the Front and Back pieces WS together and sew the shoulder seams, leaving a 9" (23cm) neck opening in the center.

Cuffs

Mark 25 rows down on each side (Front and Back) of the shoulder seam. With the RS facing and smaller needles, pick up and k50 stitches between the markers. Work in k2, p2 rib for 3" (7.5cm) or desired length. Bind off in rib. Repeat on the other side.

Sew cuff and side seams.

Weave

Follow the diagram opposite for strip placement. Pick up and k6 stitches for each strip. Work in stockinette stitch for 10" (25.5cm) for each straight strip and 15" (38cm) for each spiraled strip. End each strip by threading the end through the 6 stitches, pulling it tight, and securing. Weave the strips, spiral the ends, and tack them in place, allowing the sides of the strips to curl and form tubes.

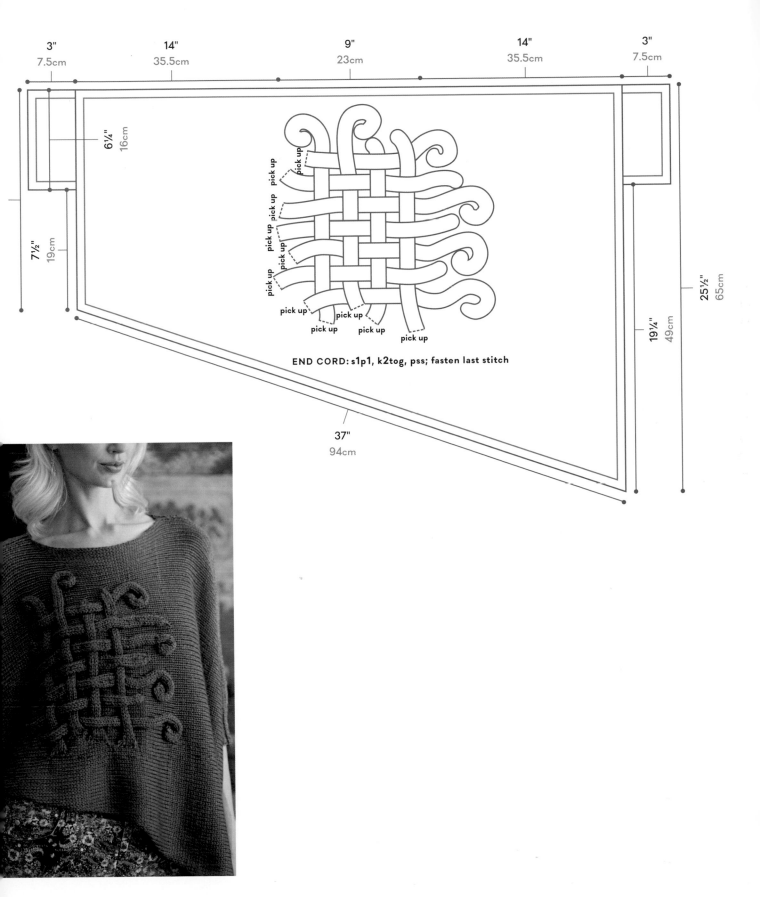

3"
7.5cm

14"
35.5cm

9"
23cm

14"
35.5cm

3"
7.5cm

6¼"
16cm

7½"
19cm

25½"
65cm

19¼"
49cm

pick up

END CORD: s1p1, k2tog, pss; fasten last stitch

37"
94cm

CHAOS COUTURE
pullover

Splendid textural yarn and braiding create this dazzling pullover that is one of a kind, thanks to a variety of different yarns that are hand-tied together. The combination of knitted details—the braided sleeve, diagonal ribbed treatment, and cable edgings—takes this design in a new direction. If you are substituting different yarns, be aware that combining a cohesive mix of yarn textures will add to the overall richness of this look.

reimagine it
It is hard to consider using a different yarn since the beautiful textural variety of the Prism yarns adds to the bold depth of the braided sleeve. (Any piece knit using Prism yarns will always be a one-of-a-kind sweater!) The slanted rib at the bottom edge could be lengthened and belted, or worked in a mix of fun colors.

SIZES

S (M, L), shown in size M

FINISHED MEASUREMENTS

Bust: 39½ (46¾, 55½)"
[100 (118.5, 141)cm]

Length: 18¼ (19, 19½)"
[46.5 (48.5, 49.5)cm]

GAUGE

20 stitches and 28 rows = 4"
(10cm) in stockinette stitch using
size U.S. 6 (4mm) needles with
yarn A

Approximately 18 stitches and
24 rows = 4" (10cm) in stockinette
stitch using size U.S. 8 (5mm)
needles with yarn B (yarn is a mix
of textured yarn so the gauge varies
throughout the skein)

12 stitches and 16 rows = 4"
(10cm) in stockinette stitch using
size U.S. 10 (6mm) needles with
yarn C

Take time to check gauge.

MATERIALS

Prism Symphony (80% merino,
10% cashmere, 10% nylon), 2 oz
(57g), 118 yd (108m); 7 (8, 9)
balls of Mushroom (A)

Prism Layers Stuff (rayon, cotton,
nylon, kid mohair, bamboo, Tencel,
wool, cashmere), 6–8 oz (170–
226g), 300 yd (274m); 1 (1, 1)
ball of Mushroom (B)

Prism Plume (100% nylon), 2.8 oz
(79g), 45 yd (41m); 2 (2, 3) balls
of Mushroom (C)

Size U.S. 6 (4mm) straight needles,
or size needed to obtain gauge

Size U.S. 8 (5mm) needles, or size
needed to obtain gauge

Size U.S. 10 (6mm) needles, or size
needed to obtain gauge

Cable needle

Stitch markers

4 stitch holders

Waste yarn for provisional cast on

Tapestry needle

Notes

• Yoke depth and sleeve width are
approximate since the braids are
elastic. The bust is based on the
stockinette stitch gauge. The
cables draw the fabric in to create
gathers.

• Sleeves and yoke are made
in strips and then braided to
shape one piece for the sleeves,
shoulders, and neck opening.

Diagonal Wave Rib

(multiple of 6 stitches + 3)
3/3 RPC: Slip 3 to cn and hold
in back, k3, p3 from cn.
Rows 1, 3, and 5 (RS): K3, *p3,
k3; repeat from * to the end.
Rows 2 and 4: P3, *k3, p3; repeat
from * to the end.
Row 6 *3/3 RPC; repeat from *

to the last 3 stitches, k3.
Rows 7, 9, and 11: P3, *k3, p3;
repeat from * to the end.
Rows 8 and 10: k3, *p3, k3;
repeat from * to the end.
Row 12: P3, *3/3 RPC; repeat
from * to the end.
Repeat rows 1–12 for pattern.

FRONT

With smallest needles and A, cast on 99 (117, 129) stitches. Work 18 rows in Diagonal Wave Rib.

Work in stockinette stitch until the piece measures 5½ (6, 6½)" [14 (15, 16.5)cm] from the cast-on edge, ending with a WS row.

Row 1 (RS): K14 (20, 26), place marker, work Diagonal Wave Rib over the next 21 stitches, place marker, k29 (35, 35), place marker, work Diagonal Wave Rib over the next 21 stitches, k14 (20, 26).

Rows 2–24: Work in patterns as established.

Work 12 rows in stockinette stitch.

Armhole Shaping

Mark the center 27 stitches. Continuing in stockinette stitch, work 12 rows of Diagonal Wave Rib over the center 27 stitches. *At the same time,* after 6 rows, bind off 3 (5, 7) stitches at the beginning of the next 2 rows, then 2 (2, 3) stitches at the beginning of the next 4 rows— 85 (99, 103) stitches.
Bind off.

BACK

Make same as the Front.

FRONT/BACK SLEEVES AND YOKE

Note: This piece starts with the sleeves on the left side, divides into two side strips to accommodate the braid, is worked across the yoke, down the right side, and joined to end at the opposite cuff.

Left Side

With medium needles and A, cast on 51 (57, 63) stitches. Work 18 rows in Diagonal Wave Rib. Work 6 (6, 4) rows in stockinette stitch.

Increase row (RS): K1, m1, knit to the last stitch, m1, k1.

Continuing in stockinette stitch, repeat Increase row every 6th (6th, 4th) row 3 (3, 5) more times—59 (65, 75) stitches. Purl 1 WS row.

Dividing row (RS): K7 (10, 15), attach a second ball of A and k45, place these 45 stitches on a holder, k7 (10, 15).

Working both sides of the sleeve at the same time, continue to work Increase row every 6th row at the outside edges 10 more times—17 (20, 25) stitches each side.

Work even on both sides until the sleeve measures 17" (43cm) or the desired length to the underarm. *Make note of the number of rows worked so it can be repeated on the other side.*

Armhole Shaping

Bind off 3 (5, 7) stitches at each armhole edge, then 1 stitch every other row 2 (2, 3) times—12 (13, 15) stitches each side.

Yoke

Work even in stockinette stitch on both sides for the front and back yokes for 18½ (22, 24¼)" [47 (56, 61.5)cm].

Right Side

At each armhole edge, increase 1 stitch every RS row 2 (2, 3) times, then cast on 3 (5, 7) stitches—17 (20, 25) stitches each side.

Work the same number of rows noted from the first sleeve.

Decrease row (RS): K1, k2tog, knit to the last 3 stitches of the other side, ssk, k1.

Repeat Decrease row every 6th row 9 more times. Work 3 rows in stockinette stitch.

Joining row (RS): K7 (10, 15), cast on (preferably with a provisional cast on) 45 stitches, k7 (10, 15)—59 (65, 75) stitches.

Continue decreasing 1 stitch at each outside edge every 6th row 4 (4, 1) more time(s), then every 4th row 0 (0, 5) times—51 (57, 63) stitches.

Work 6 (6, 4) rows even in stockinette stitch.

Work 18 rows in Diagonal Wave Rib.

Bind off in rib.

CENTER SLEEVE AND YOKE STRIPS

Notes: The number of rows worked in each strip differ because of yarn variations. Knit each strip to the indicated length, ending all strips with a WS row.

LEFT SIDE

Strip 1

With the RS facing, place the rightmost 11 stitches onto medium-size needles. With B, k1, m1, k9, m1, k1—13 stitches. Work in seed stitch for 23 (26, 28)" [58.5 (66, 71)cm] as follows:

Row 1: K1, *p1, k1; repeat from * to end.

Repeat row 1 for pattern.

Place stitches on a holder.

Strip 2

With the RS facing, place the next 10 stitches onto the largest needles.

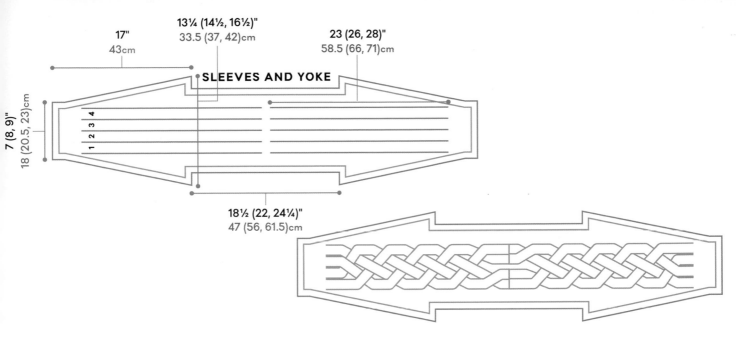

SLEEVES AND YOKE

17"
43cm

13¼ (14½, 16½)"
33.5 (37, 42)cm

23 (26, 28)"
58.5 (66, 71)cm

7 (8, 9)"
18 (20.5, 23)cm

18½ (22, 24¼)"
47 (56, 61.5)cm

With C, k1, m1, k8, m1, k1—12 stitches.

Work in reverse stockinette stitch (purl on RS, knit on WS) for 23 (26, 28)" [58.5 (66, 71)cm]. Place stitches on a holder.

Strip 3

With the RS facing, place the next 13 stitches onto the smallest needles.

With A, work in stockinette stitch for 23 (26, 28)" [58.5 (66, 71) cm].

Place on a holder.

Strip 4

With the RS facing, place the last 11 stitches onto the medium-size needles.

With B, k1, m1, k9, m1, k1—13 stitches.

Work in stockinette stitch for 23 (26, 28)" [58.5 (66, 71)cm]. Place on a holder.

Braiding

Following the diagram (right), braid the 4 strips together. Pin

and sew them to the inner sleeve edges. Twisting 2 strips each for the front and back yokes, pin in place and set aside.

RIGHT SIDE

Remove the waste yarn, and work the strips the same as the left side. When dividing strips for the yoke, make sure to match the ones from the left side, adding or removing rows as necessary to meet at the center neck edge. Pin in place.

FINISHING

Graft the strips using Kitchener stitch (see page 170) and sew them to the sleeve and yoke side strips.

Mark the center 9" (23cm) for the neck opening and tack the strips together at each side.

Sew the sleeve seams. Sew the side seams.

Sew the front and back yoke edges to the Front and Back, matching underarm shaping.

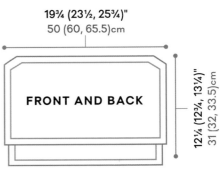

19¾ (23½, 25¾)"
50 (60, 65.5)cm

FRONT AND BACK

12¼ (12¾, 13¼)"
31 (32, 33.5)cm

SLEEVE BRAIDING

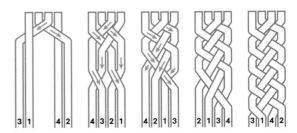

chapter 4

STITCH IMPACT

This chapter includes interesting and unique stitches, color work, and edgings that all go beyond "business as usual" stitches. By that I mean they jump out and shout, "Look how special I am!" Within these patterns you'll find a lovely repeat tuck stitch, a bulky knit bold leaf stitch, and two exciting motifs—a dressage horse and a scary skull spirit. Edgier versions of traditional stitches include an unusual use of Fair Isle knitting and a cool slant using a scalloped edging. Adding such elements to a design transforms a garment into something far from ordinary. I hope you enjoy knitting and wearing these bold fashion statements as much as I do.

SPRING
FORWARD
dress or tunic

Big needles, big yarn, big bold stitches, and a fabulous dress (or tunic) that takes little time and effort. What could be more fun and creatively rewarding? Spring Forward features flattering, bold lines that update a classic knitted leaf. The shape is knit in two pieces from the bottom up to the bodice, and the sleeves are made up to the armholes. Then all four pieces are placed on one circular needle and knit in a rib pattern with graduated decreases to shape the yoke. Be prepared to hear, "Wow! Where did you get it?"

reimagine it
Consider making a shorter version and continuing the neckline to create a cowl neck. Cascade Yarns also offers Magnum Print (a multicolor version of Magnum), which can be used for a completely different look. Or combine that print with a solid yoke and a multicolor bottom.

SKILL LEVEL

TIME

SIZES

S/M (L/XL), *shown in size S/M*

FINISHED MEASUREMENTS

Bust: 36 (45)" [91 (114)cm]

Overall length: 30¼ (32¼)"
[77 (82)cm]

GAUGE

8 stitches and 12 rows = 4" (10cm)
in stockinette stitch

Take time to check gauge.

MATERIALS

Cascade Magnum (100% Peruvian
highland wool), 8.8 oz (250g),
123 yd (112m); 6 (7) skeins of
#2422 Orchid

Size U.S. 15 (10mm) straight
needles and 24" (61cm) circular
needle, or size needed to obtain
gauge

Stitch markers (optional)

Stitch holders

Matching worsted-weight wool for
seaming

Tapestry needle

Row 19: Ssk, k1, k2tog—3
stitches.

Row 21: Sk2p—1 stitch.
There are 2 stitches decreased
after each leaf is complete.

FRONT

Cast on 54 (62) stitches.

Row 1 (RS): K2, *p2, k2; repeat
from * to end.

Row 2: P2, *k2, p2; repeat from
* to end.

Row 3: Purl.

Row 4: K26 (30), k2tog, k26
(30)—53 (61) stitches.

Row 5: P10 (14), k1, [p7, k1] 4
times, p10 (14).

Row 6: K10 (14), p1, [k7, p1] 4
times, k10 (14).

Rows 7–24 (7–30): Repeat rows
5 and 6.

At the same time, decrease every
16th row 4 times as follows:

Decrease row (RS): P1, p2tog tbl,
work to the last 3 stitches,
p2tog, p1.

Note: See photographs for leaf
placement on the dress. The
leaves are numbered 1 through
5 from right to left. The single
columns of RS knits are the stems
on which leaves will be knit.

Work leaves on stems 1 and 5 as
follows:

Leaves 1 and 5 setup rows (RS):

Leaf Pattern

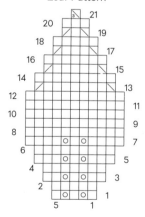

Stitch Key

☐ K on RS, P on WS

⊡ Yarn over (yo)

◿ K2tog on RS, p2tog on WS

◺ Ssk on RS, p2tog tbl on WS

◩ Sk2p

Leaf Pattern
(begins with 3 stitches)

Row 1: K1, yo, k1, yo, k1—5
stitches.

Row 2 and all WS rows: Purl.

Row 3: K2, yo, k1, yo, k2—7
stitches.

Row 5: K3, yo, k1, yo, k 3—9
stitches.

Row 7: K4, yo, k1, yo, k4—11
stitches.

Rows 9 and 11: Knit.

Row 13: Ssk, k7, k2tog–9 stitches.

Row 15: Ssk, k5, k2tog—7
stitches.

Row 17: Ssk, k3, k2tog—5
stitches.

Work to 1 stitch before stem 1, work row 1 of Leaf pattern over the next 3 stitches, work to 1 stitch before stem 5, work row 1 of Leaf pattern over the next 3 stitches, work to the end. (If desired, place markers before and after Leaf pattern stitches.) Continue in patterns and decreases as established, ending with row 4 of Leaf pattern.

Leaf 3 setup row: Work in patterns as established to 1 stitch before stem 3, work row 1 of Leaf pattern, work in patterns as established to the end.

Continue in patterns and decreases as established, ending with row 16 of Leaf 3.

Leaf 2 setup row: Work in patterns as established to 1 stitch before stem 2, work row 1 of Leaf pattern over the next 3 stitches, work in patterns as established to the end.

Continue in patterns and decreases as established, ending with row 6 of Leaf 2.

Leaf 4 setup row: Work in patterns as established to 1 stitch before stem 4, work row 1 of Leaf pattern over the next 3 stitches, work in patterns as established to the end.

When the last Leaf is complete, ending with a WS row, [purl 1 row,

knit 1 row] twice, decreasing 0 (1) stitch on the last WS row—36 (42) stitches.

Place 36 (42) stitches on a holder.

BACK

Work same as the Front.

RIGHT SLEEVE

Cast on 18 (22) stitches.

Row 1 (RS): K2, *p2, k2; repeat from * to end.

Row 2: P2, *k2, p2; repeat from * to end.

Row 3: P9 (11), m1p, p9 (11)—19 (23) stitches.

Row 4: Knit.

Row 5: P9 (11), k1, p9 (11).

Row 6: K9 (11), p1, k9 (11).

Rows 7 and 8 (7–10): Repeat rows 5 and 6.

At the same time, increase every 6th row 4 times as follows:

Increase row (RS): P1, m1p, work to the last stitch, m1p, p1—27 (31) stitches.

Begin Leaf pattern on RS center k1.

Leaf setup row 9 (11): Work to 1 stitch before the stem, work row 1 of Leaf pattern, work to the end. Continue in patterns and increases as established until sleeve measures 16 (17)" [40.5

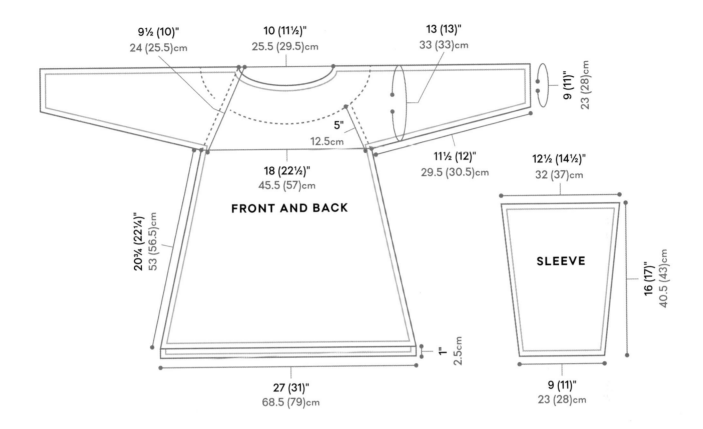

9½ (10)"
24 (25.5)cm

10 (11½)"
25.5 (29.5)cm

13 (13)"
33 (33)cm

9 (11)"
23 (28)cm

5"
12.5cm

18 (22½)"
45.5 (57)cm

FRONT AND BACK

11½ (12)"
29.5 (30.5)cm

12½ (14½)"
32 (37)cm

20¾ (22¼)"
53 (56.5)cm

SLEEVE

16 (17)"
40.5 (43)cm

1"
2.5cm

27 (31)"
68.5 (79)cm

9 (11)"
23 (28)cm

(43)cm], ending with a WS row—25 (29) stitches. Place stitches on a holder.

LEFT SLEEVE

Work same as the Right Sleeve, starting the Leaf pattern 9" (23cm) from the cast-on edge.

YOKE

Place stitches onto the circular needle, ready to begin a WS row. Starting at the center back, place 18 (21) Back stitches, 25 (29) Left Sleeve stitches, 36 (42) Front stitches, 25 (29)

Right Sleeve stitches, 18 (21) Back stitches onto the circular needle—122 (142) stitches. Beginning with a WS row, work back and forth as follows:

Row 1 (WS): P2, *k2, p2; repeat from * to end.

Row 2: K2, *p2, k2; repeat from * to end.

Row 3: Repeat row 1.

Row 4: K2, *p2, k2tog; repeat from * to the last 4 stitches, p2, k2—93 (108) stitches.

Row 5: P2, *k2, p1; repeat from * to the last 4 stitches, k2, p2.

Rows 6–9: Work in rib as established.

Row 10: K2, *p2tog, k1; repeat from * to the last stitch, k1—63 (73) stitches.

Row 11: P2, *k1, p1; repeat from * to the last stitch, p1.

Rows 12–15: Work in rib as established.

Bind off in pattern.

FINISHING

With matching worsted-weight yarn, sew the top 9½ (10)" [24 (25.5)cm] at each side of the Sleeves to the Front and Back. Sew the side seams. Sew the sleeve seams.

BUTTONS AND BOWS
manteau

The colors, buttons, and tailored shape give this delightful-to-wear design a slightly vintage appeal. Although it has classic knit shaping, using the tuck stitch texture makes it new and interesting. This versatile design can be worn as either a dress or a jacket. If you'd like, the bows can be omitted and the waist belted. As you can see, this piece has a lot of stockinette stitch along with the entertaining tucks, and though not difficult, it is a time-consuming piece.

reimagine it
Think about choosing a color for the tucked bottom section and switching to a contrasting color at the beginning of the waist darts. Then choose a third color for the collar and bows. Remove bows or add even more to create the look you want. The piece could also be easily converted into a shorter cardigan style.

SKILL LEVEL

TIME

SIZES

S (M/L, XL), *shown in size M/L*

FINISHED MEASUREMENTS

Bust: 39¼ (45½, 58)" [99.5 (115.5, 147.5)cm]

Overall length: 31 (32, 33)" [79 (81, 84)cm]

Sleeve length to underarm: 10 (10½, 11)" [25.5 (26.5, 28)cm]

GAUGE

20 stitches and 28 rows = 4" (10cm) in stockinette stitch on larger needles

Take time to check gauge.

MATERIALS

Kollage Milky Whey (50% milk, 50% soy), 1¾ oz (50g), 137 yd (123m); 9 (12, 16) balls of #7610 Milky Green (A); 2 (2, 3) balls of #7604 Cameo (B)

Size U.S. 6 (4mm) straight needles, or size needed to obtain gauge

Size U.S. 4 (3.5mm) set of 5 double-pointed needles

Stitch markers

Removable stitch markers

Stitch holders

Tapestry needle

Eight ¾" (2cm) buttons (JHB's #12594)

5 sew-on snaps (optional)

LEFT FRONT

With larger needles and B, cast on 55 (75, 95) stitches.

Hem

Work in stockinette stitch for 1" (2.5cm), ending with a WS row. Change to A and knit 3 rows. Work in Tuck Stitch pattern as follows:

Rows 1–16: Work in stockinette stitch.

Row 17 (RS): K15, *k5, insert the dpn through these 5 stitches on the WS, k15; repeat from * to end. Place a marker in the last stitch on the WS.

Rows 18–26: Work 9 rows in stockinette stitch.

Row 27: K15, *knit the next 5 stitches together with the 5 stitches from the dpn below, k15; repeat from * to end, knitting the last stitch together with the marked stitch below.

Rows 28–44: Work 17 rows in stockinette stitch.

Row 45: K5, *k5, insert a dpn through the back of these 5 stitches, k15; repeat from * to the last 5 stitches, k5. Place a marker in the last stitch on the WS.

Rows 46–54: Work 9 rows in stockinette stitch.

Row 55: K5, *knit the next 5 stitches together with the 5 stitches from the dpn below, k15; repeat from * to the last 10 stitches, knit the next 5 stitches together with the 5 stitches from the dpn below, k4, knit the last stitch together with the marked stitch below.

Row 56: Purl.

Repeat rows 1–56 once, then work rows 1–44 once more.

Shape Waist

Row 1: K15, *ssk, k1, k2tog, k15; repeat from * to end—51 (69, 87) stitches.

Rows 2 and 4: Purl.

Row 3: K14, *ssk, k1, k2tog, k13; repeat from * to the last 14 stitches, k14—47 (63, 79) stitches.

Row 5: K13, *ssk, k1, k2tog, k11; repeat from * to the last 13 stitches, k13—43 (57, 71) stitches.

Work even in stockinette stitch for 4 (4½, 5)" [10 (11.5, 12.5)cm], ending with a WS row.

Shape Armhole

Next row (RS): Bind off 3 (5, 8) stitches, knit to the end—40 (52, 63) stitches.

Next row: Purl 1 row.

Decrease row (RS): K1, k2tog, knit to the end—39 (51, 62) stitches. Repeat Decrease row every RS row 2 (2, 8) more times—37 (49, 54) stitches.

Work even in stockinette stitch until armhole measures 5 (5½, 6)" [12.5 (14, 15)cm], ending with a RS row.

Neck Shaping

At the beginning of WS rows at the neck edge, bind off 10 (12, 14) stitches once, 2 stitches 3 (4, 5) times, then 1 stitch 2 (2, 3)

times—19 (27, 27) stitches. Work even in stockinette stitch until armhole measures 8 (8½, 9)" [20.5 (21.5, 23)cm]. Place shoulder stitches on a holder.

RIGHT FRONT

With larger needles and B, cast on 55 (75, 95) stitches.

Hem

Work in stockinette stitch for 1" (2.5cm), ending with a WS row. Change to A and knit 3 rows. Work in Tuck Stitch pattern as follows:

Rows 1–16: Work in stockinette stitch.

Row 17 (RS): Place a marker in the first stitch on the WS. K15, *k5, insert a dpn through the back of these 5 stitches, k15; repeat from * to end.

Rows 18–26: Work 9 rows in stockinette stitch.

Row 27: Knit the first stitch together with the marked stitch below, k14, *knit the next 5 stitches together with the 5 stitches from the dpn below, k15; repeat from * to end.

Rows 28–44: Work 17 rows in stockinette stitch.

Row 45: Place a marker in the first stitch on the WS. K5, *k5, insert a dpn through the back of these 5 stitches, k15; repeat from * to the last 5 stitches, k5.

Rows 46–54: Work 9 rows in stockinette stitch.

Row 55: Knit the first stitch together with the marked stitch below, k4, *knit the next 5 stitches together with the 5 stitches from the dpn below, k15; repeat from * to the last 10 stitches, knit the next 5 stitches together with the 5 stitches from the dpn below, k4, knit the last stitch together with the marked stitch below.

Row 56: Purl.

Repeat rows 1–56 once, then work rows 1–44 once more. Work same as the Left Front until the armhole shaping, ending with a RS row.

Shape Armhole

Next row (WS): Bind off 3 (5, 8) stitches, purl to end.

Decrease row (RS): Knit to the last 3 stitches, ssk, k1.

Repeat Decrease row every RS row 2 (2, 8) times more—37 (49, 54) stitches.

Work even in stockinette stitch until armhole measures 5 (5½, 6)" [12.5 (14, 15)cm], ending with a WS row.

Work neck shaping and remainder of Right Front same as Left Front,

working neck bind-offs at the beginning of RS rows.

LEFT AND RIGHT BACKS

Make Left and Right Backs same as Left and Right Fronts, omitting the neck shaping. Place 37 (49, 54) stitches on a holder.

SLEEVES

With larger needles and B, cast on 57 (61, 67) stitches.

Hem

Work in stockinette stitch for 1" (2.5cm), ending with a WS row. Change to A and knit 3 rows. Mark the center 5 stitches. Work 16 rows in stockinette stitch.

Increase row (RS): K1, m1, knit to the last stitch, m1, k1.

Repeat Increase row every 4th row 7 (8, 9) more times —73 (79, 87) stitches.

At the same time, starting on the same row as the first increase, work 3 Tuck Stitches on the center 5 stitches as follows:

Row 1 (RS): Knit to the center 5 stitches, insert a dpn through the back of these 5 stitches, knit to the end.

Rows 2–10: Work 9 rows in stockinette stitch.

Row 11: Knit to the center 5 stitches, knit the next 5 stitches together with the 5 stitches from the dpn below, knit to the end.

Rows 12–28: Work 17 rows in stockinette stitch.

Repeat rows 1–28 once, then work rows 1–11 once more.

Work even in stockinette stitch until sleeve measures 10 (10½, 11)" [25.5 (26.5, 28)cm].

Shape Sleeve Cap

Bind off 3 (5, 8) stitches at the beginning of the next 2 rows, then decrease 1 stitch each side every RS row 16 (17, 18) times. Bind off 3 stitches at the beginning of the next 8 rows. Bind off the remaining 11 stitches.

FINISHING

Sew the back seam.

Join shoulder seams using the 3-needle bind-off method (see page 169). Set in the Sleeves. Sew the side and sleeve seams. Sew hems to the wrong side.

Left Front Band

With the RS facing and A, pick up and k141 (147, 153) stitches from neck edge to the bottom edge, working through 3 layers over the tucks. Work in k3, p3 rib for 1" (2.5cm). Bind off in rib.

Right Front Band

With the RS facing and A, pick up and k141 (147, 153) stitches from the bottom edge to the neck edge, working through 3 layers over the tucks. Work 3 rows in k3, p3 rib.

Buttonhole row (RS): *Work 14 (15, 16) stitches, bind off 3 stitches; repeat from * 7 more times, work to the last 5 (3, 1) stitches as set.

Next row: Work in rib as established, casting on 3 stitches over the bound-off stitches of the previous row.

Continue in k3, p3 rib until rib measures 1" (2.5cm). Bind off in rib.

Sew buttons to Left Front band to correspond with buttonholes.

Neck Band

With the RS facing and smaller needles, pick up and k95 (107, 131) stitches evenly around the neck opening, including the front bands. Work in k1, p1 rib for 3½" (9cm).

Work Picot Bind-Off as follows: Bind off 2 stitches, *slip the last stitch back onto the left-hand needle, cast on 3 stitches using the cable cast-on (see page 169), bind off 5 stitches; repeat from * to the last stitch, bind off the last stitch.

Lace Ruffle Collar (optional)

With larger needles and B, cast on 295 (323, 379) stitches (a multiple of 14 stitches plus 1 more).

Row 1 and all WS rows: Purl.

Rows 2, 4, 6, 8, 10, and 12: K1, *yo, k3, ssk, yo, sk2p, yo, k2tog, k3, yo, k1; repeat from * to end.

Row 14: K1, *k2tog; repeat from * to end—148 (162, 190) stitches.

Row 16: P1, [k1, p1] twice, *k2 (2, 2) ssk; repeat from * to the last 7 (5, 5) stitches, k2 (0, 0), [p1, k1] twice, p1—114 (124, 145) stitches.

Row 17: Purl, decreasing 11 (7, 10) stitches evenly between the

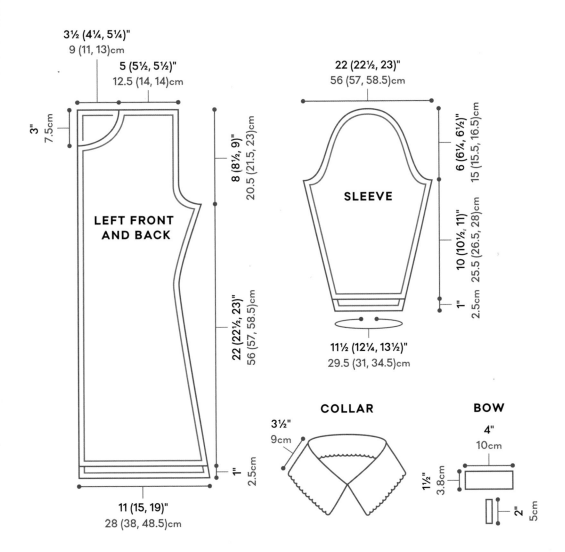

3½ (4¼, 5¼)"
9 (11, 13)cm

5 (5½, 5½)"
12.5 (14, 14)cm

22 (22½, 23)"
56 (57, 58.5)cm

3"
7.5cm

LEFT FRONT AND BACK

8 (8½, 9)"
20.5 (21.5, 23)cm

22 (22½, 23)"
56 (57, 58.5)cm

1"
2.5cm

11 (15, 19)"
28 (38, 48.5)cm

SLEEVE

6 (6¼, 6½)"
15 (15.5, 16.5)cm

10 (10½, 11)"
25.5 (26.5, 28)cm

1"
2.5cm

11½ (12¼, 13½)"
29.5 (31, 34.5)cm

COLLAR

3½"
9cm

BOW

4"
10cm

1½"
3.8cm

2"
5cm

two sets of rib stitches—103 (117, 135) stitches.
Work in k1, p1 rib across all stitches for 1" (2.5cm). Bind off in rib.

Sew 5 snaps evenly across the edge of the collar and around the neck band to attach it.

Bow (MAKE 3)
With larger needles and B, cast on 15 stitches.
Work in k1, p1 rib for 4" (10cm). Bind off in rib.

Tie (MAKE 3)
With larger needles and B, cast on 5 stitches.
Work in k1, p1 rib for 1½" (3.8cm). Bind off in rib.

Wrap the tie around the center of the bow and sew the bound-off edge to the cast-on edge.
Notes: Adjust the fit of this jacket by connecting 2 adjacent darts (waist decrease points) and sewing a bow over each join. Make a pleat between the front decrease darts and attach a bow on each side. Make one pleat at center back and attach bow.

DRESSAGE PONY
poncholette

Any horse lover would be happy wearing this piece, sporting a classic jumping horse and other sophisticated details. The main feature is the horse motif that can either be knitted in or worked in duplicate stitch after the piece is knit. The triple cuff detail includes a rolled edge, a rib, and a two-color houndstooth pattern. An I-cord drawstring calls attention to one side, and an elegant braided cord collar at the neck adds extra interest to this universally flattering style.

reimagine it
Sans horse the piece is instantly reimagined. Omitting the horse will give you a subtler look, and you can still keep the comfy fit and casual style of the design. Instead of the horse, you can also add any motif of your choice, for example, a flower or a cat. The shape provides the perfect canvas for you to reimagine this stylish design.

TIME

SIZE

One size

FINISHED MEASUREMENTS

Bust: Oversized 58½" (148.6cm)

Overall length (including waist ribbing): 24½" (62.2cm)

Sleeve length to underarm: 12½" (31.7cm)

GAUGE

20 stitches and 28 rows = 4" (10cm) in stockinette stitch on larger needles

Take time to check gauge.

MATERIALS

Aslan Trends Royal Alpaca (100% alpaca), 3½ oz (100g), 220 yd (200m); 5 balls of #6365 Sable (A); 2 balls of #19 Black (B); 1 ball of #1570 Pale Blue (C)

Size U.S. 7 (4.5mm) 24" (61cm) circular needle, or size needed to obtain gauge

Size U.S. 5 (3.75mm) double-pointed needles

Stitch markers

Tapestry needle

Waste yarn

Safety pin

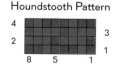

Color Key
■ B
■ A
□ Repeat

Houndstooth Pattern

Houndstooth Check Pattern

Row 1 (RS): K1 B, *k1 A, k3 B; repeat from * to the last 3 stitches, k1 A, k2 B.

Row 2: *P3 A, p1 B; repeat from * to end.

Row 3: *K3 A, k1 B; repeat from * to end.

Row 4: P1 B, *p1 A, p3 B; repeat from * to the last 3 stitches, p1 A, p2 B.

Repeat rows 1–4 for pattern.

Note: This garment is knit from side to side. Read ahead as multiple shapings occur at the same time. The silhouette of the horse is worked in duplicate stitch, or can be knitted in intarsia (see page 170) instead.

BACK

Starting with B and larger needle, at the right back sleeve, cast on 30 stitches. Work 9 rows in stockinette stitch.

Shoulder increase row (RS): K1, m1, knit to end.

Continuing in stockinette stitch, repeat Shoulder increase row every 10th row 10 more times. *At the same time*, when sleeve measures 4" (10cm), ending with a WS row, increase on next and every RS row 6 times as follows:

Underarm increase row (RS): Work to the last stitch, m1, k1—40 stitches for body.

After all underarm increases have been completed, cast on 70 stitches for body using the cable cast-on method (see page 169) at the beginning of the next WS row.

Work 43 rows in stockinette stitch, continuing shoulder increases as established, ending with a WS row—117 stitches. Change to C and work 20 rows even in stockinette stitch.

Change to A and work 10 rows even in stockinette stitch.

Back Neck
Place a marker at the shoulder edge, work 59 rows even in stockinette stitch, place marker at the next shoulder edge.
Shoulder decrease row (RS): K1, k2tog, knit to end.
Continuing in stockinette stitch, repeat Shoulder decrease row every 10th row 10 more times.
At the same time, when piece measures 24½" (62.2cm) from the body cast on, work bottom curve on WS rows as follows: Bind off 1 stitch every WS row 6 times, 1 stitch every 4th WS row 5 times, then bind off 59 stitches for body—40 stitches.
Underarm decrease row (RS): Work to the last 3 stitches, ssk, k1. Repeat Underarm decrease row every RS row 5 more times—34 stitches.
When all shoulder decreases have been worked, work 9 rows even in stockinette stitch on 30 stitches.
Bind off.

FRONT
Starting at the right front sleeve, with B and larger needle, cast

on 30 stitches. Work 9 rows in stockinette stitch.

Shoulder increase row (RS): Knit to the last stitch, m1, k1.

Continuing in stockinette stitch, repeat Shoulder increase row every 10th row 10 more times.

At the same time, when sleeve measures 4" (10cm), ending with a WS row, increase on next and every RS row 6 times as follows:

Underarm increase row (RS): K1, m1, work to the last stitch.

After all underarm increases have been completed, cast on 70 stitches for body using the cable method at the beginning of the next RS row.

Work 43 rows in stockinette stitch, continuing shoulder increases as established, ending with a WS row—117 stitches.

Change to C and work 20 rows even in stockinette stitch.

Change to A and work 10 rows even in stockinette stitch.

Front Neck Shaping

Decrease row (RS): Knit to the last 3 stitches, ssk, k1.

Repeat Decrease row every RS row twice more, then every 4th row 3 more times—111 stitches.

Work 26 rows even in stockinette stitch.

Increase row (RS): Knit to the last stitch, m1, k1.

Repeat Increase row every 4th row twice more, then every RS row 3 more times—117 stitches. Purl 1 WS row.

Shoulder decrease row (RS): Knit to the last 3 stitches, ssk, k1. Continuing in stockinette stitch, repeat Shoulder decrease row every 10th row 10 more times. *At the same time,* when piece measures 24½" (62.2cm) from the body cast-on, shape the bottom curve, then the underarm, on RS rows as follows:

Bind off 1 stitch every RS row 6 times, 1 stitch every 4th row 5 times, then bind off 59 body stitches.

Underarm decrease row (RS): K1, k2tog, work to end.

Repeat Underarm decrease row every RS row 5 more times. When all shoulder decreases have been worked, work 9 rows even in stockinette stitch on 30 stitches.

Bind off.

With B, work Dressage Pony chart on the Front in duplicate stitch (see page 169), starting the first stitch of the chart in the 3rd stitch from the ribbing and the first row in the C section.

SLEEVES

Sew Front to Back from cast on to neck edge.

With the RS facing, larger needle, and B, pick up 60 stitches evenly along the sleeve edge. Work 12 rows in Houndstooth Check pattern. Keeping the needle in the stitches, thread waste yarn through the stitches for later use.

Next row (RS): With B, knit. Work in k2, p2 rib for 1½" (3.8cm). Bind off.

Place the stitches on the waste yarn onto larger needle, ready to work a WS row.

With C, purl 1 WS row.

Decrease row (RS): K1, k2tog, knit to the last 3 stitches, ssk, k1. Continuing in stockinette stitch, repeat Decrease row every 4th row 8 more times—42 stitches. Bind off. Repeat for second sleeve.

FINISHING

LOWER EDGE RIB
Front

With the RS facing and matching colors across the bottom edge, with B and larger needles pick up 39 stitches, with C pick up 18 stitches, and with A pick up 117 stitches—174 stitches. Work in k2, p2 rib in established colors for 1" (2.5cm). Bind off.

Back

With the RS facing and matching colors across the bottom edge, with A and larger needles pick up 117 stitches, with C pick up 18 stitches, and with B pick up 39 stitches—174 stitches. Work in k2, p2 rib in established colors for 1" (2.5cm). Bind off.

SIDE CASING
Front

With the RS facing, larger needles, and A, starting at the rib edge, pick up 6 stitches along the side edge of the rib and 33 stitches across the bound-off stitches—39 stitches.

Knit 1 WS row.

Knit 1 RS row. Continue in stockinette stitch until casing measures ¾" (2cm) from the pickup. Bind off.

Back

With the RS facing, larger needle, and A, starting at the 33rd bound-off stitch from the left, pick up 33 stitches across the bound-off stitches and 6 stitches along the side edge of the rib—39 stitches.

Knit 1 WS row.

Knit 1 RS row. Continue in stockinette stitch until casing measures ¾" (2cm) from the pickup. Bind off.

Pony Chart

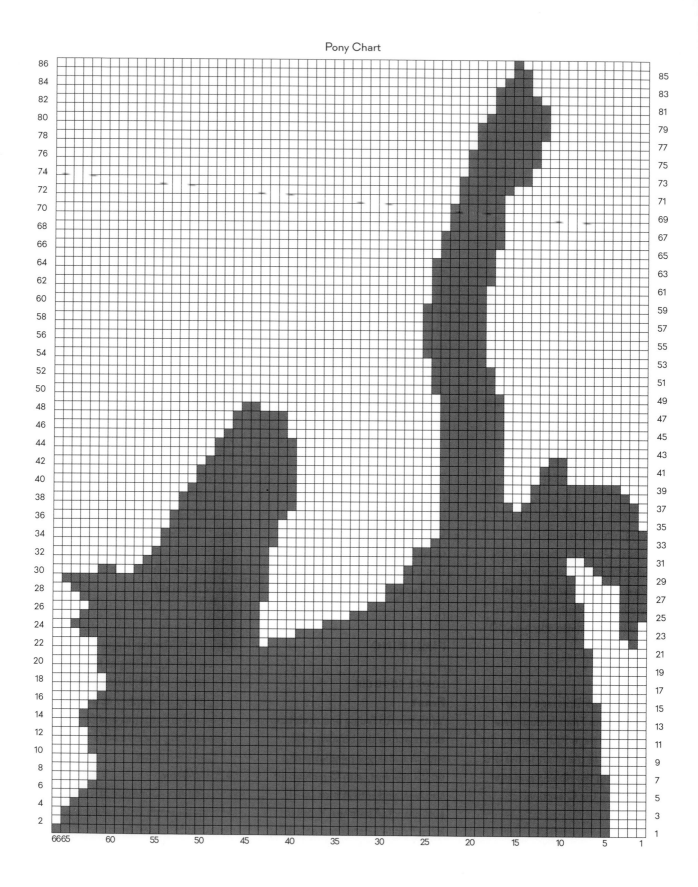

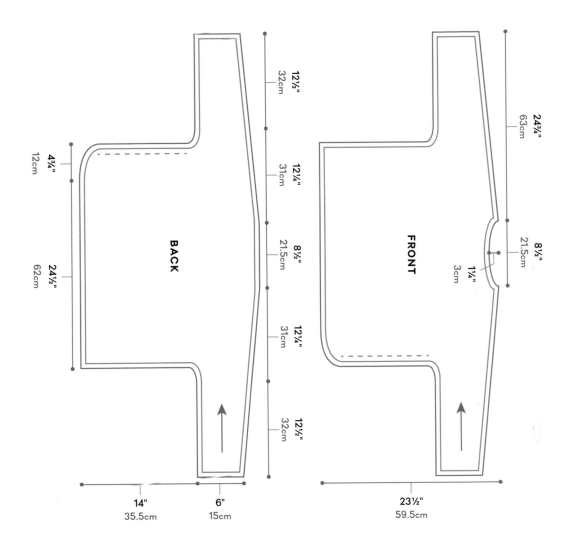

BACK

12½"
32cm

12¼"
31cm

8½"
21.5cm

12¼"
31cm

12½"
32cm

4¾"
12cm

24½"
62cm

14"
35.5cm

6"
15cm

FRONT

24¾"
63cm

8½"
21.5cm

1¼"
3cm

23½"
59.5cm

Sew underarm and side seams. Fold Front and Back casings to the WS and sew in place.

I-cord (MAKE 2)

With dpns and A, cast on 3 stitches. *Do not turn work. Slide the stitches to the other end of the needle, k3; repeat from * until cord measures 30" (76cm). K3tog and fasten off.

Attach a safety pin to one end and insert an I-cord through each casing. Secure the tops of the I-cords to the casing and knot the ends of the cords.

NECK BAND

With A, cast on 21 stitches. Work in k1, p1 rib for 6½" (16.5cm), ending with a WS row.

Next row (RS): *Work 7 stitches in rib, join another strand of A; repeat from * once, work 7 stitches in rib.

Work each strip separately in stockinette stitch for 6" (15cm), ending with a WS row.

Braid these three separate strips together, ending with the first strand ready to work a RS row.

Joining row (RS): With the first strand of yarn, k21, dropping the other strands of yarn.

Continue across all stitches in k1, p1 rib for 6½" (16.5cm). Bind off. Sew cast-on edge to bound-off edge. Center the cable at the front neck and sew in place.

SPIRITS FLY
pullover

An admittedly faux Goth look, the shape and fit of this piece is one of my favorites. The extra-deep raglan sleeve is quite flattering. The skull, crosses, and edging motifs are created with duplicate stitch, so you can also create this piece with or without the motifs. The yarn used for the background creates a wonderful uneven striping that is beautiful on its own, but also makes the perfect background for the skull spirit. Although made with easy stockinette stitch, this piece requires a lot of knitting and some advanced color work. Let your needles fly!

reimagine it
Anything goes here. Reimagine this basic shape without the motifs, give it a different background color, and add stitch patterns or your own motif or two if you wish.

TIME

SIZE

One size

FINISHED MEASUREMENTS

Bust: 54" (137cm)

Overall length: 30" (76cm)

Sleeve length: 12½" (32cm)

GAUGE

16 stitches and 24 rows = 4" (10cm) in stockinette stitch

Take time to check gauge.

Note: Skull motif is worked in duplicate stitch after the piece is knit.

MATERIALS

Cascade Casablanca (60% wool, 25% silk, 15% mohair), 3½ oz (100g), 220 yd (201m); 5 skeins of #12 Jemstones (A)

Cascade Lana D'Oro, (50% alpaca, 50% wool) 3½ oz (100g), 219 yd (200m); 1 ball each of #1055 Black (B), #1086 Hare (C), and #1089 Dark Grey and Medium Grey Twist (D)

Cascade 220 Heathers (100% Peruvian highland wool), 3½ oz (100g), 220 yd (201m); 1 skein each of #2425 Provence (E) and #2450 Mystic Purple (F)

Plymouth 24K (82% nylon, 18% lamé) 1¾ oz (50g), 187 yd (171m), 1 ball of #0002 Silver (G)

Size U.S. 9 (5.5mm) straight needles, or size needed to obtain gauge

Tapestry needle

Size U.S. G-6 (4mm) crochet hook

BACK

With B, cast on 117 stitches. Starting with a WS row, work 6 rows in stockinette stitch. Knit 1 WS row for turning ridge. Work 6 rows in stockinette stitch. Continue in stockinette stitch in the following color sequence: 10 rows F, 2 rows E, 10 rows F, 12 rows B.

Change to A and work in stockinette stitch until piece measures 14" (35.5cm) from the turning ridge, ending with a WS row.

Raglan Shaping

Decrease row (RS): K1, k2tog, knit to the last 3 stitches, ssk, k1. Repeat Decrease row every RS row 5 times, every 4th row 14 times, then every RS row 20 times—37 stitches. Bind off.

FRONT

Work same as Back, ending with 12 rows of B. Change to D and work 8 rows in stockinette stitch.

Change to A and continue same as Back until 53 stitches remain, ending with a WS row.

Neck Shaping

Continue raglan shaping at armholes and *at the same time*, work as follows:

Next row (RS): Work 15 stitches, join a second ball of A, bind off the next 23 stitches, work the remaining 15 stitches to the end. Working on both sides at the same time, at each neck edge, bind off 2 stitches twice and 1 stitch once.

When all raglan shaping is complete, bind off the remaining 2 stitches on each side.

SLEEVES (MAKE 2)

With B, cast on 44 stitches. Work in K1, p1 rib for 1½" (3.8cm).

Increase row (RS): K1, *kfb; repeat from * to the last stitch, k1—86 stitches.

Work in stockinette stitch for 1" (2.5cm), ending with a WS row. Change to A.

Increase row (RS): K1, m1, knit to the last stitch, m1, k1—88 stitches.

Repeat this Increase row every RS row 13 more times—114 stitches.

Continue even in stockinette stitch until piece measures 12" (30.5cm) from the cast-on edge, ending with a WS row.

Raglan Shaping

Decrease row (RS): K1, k2tog, knit to the last 3 stitches, ssk, k1—112 stitches.

Repeat Decrease row every 4th row 9 more times, then every RS row 35 more times—24 stitches. Bind off.

COWL COLLAR

With B, cast on 115 stitches. Work in stockinette stitch in the following color sequence: 6 rows B, 10 rows F, 4 rows B, 8 rows E, 4 rows B, 22 rows A, 8 rows B, 6 rows D.

With D, knit 5 rows.

Bind off loosely.

SKULL, ARROW, AND DIAMOND MOTIFS (OPTIONAL)

Work motifs in duplicate stitch (see page 169) following the charts and referring to photographs for placement.

FINISHING

Sew raglan seams. Sew side and sleeve seams, using a full stitch at each selvedge. Fold and sew hem to WS of the garment. Sew the Collar seam. With the WS of the Collar facing the RS of the garment, pin the cast-on edge of the Collar to the neck opening. With B and the crochet hook, join them using a slip stitch (see page 171).

Chart 1

Color Key
A
B
C
D
E
F
G

Chart 3

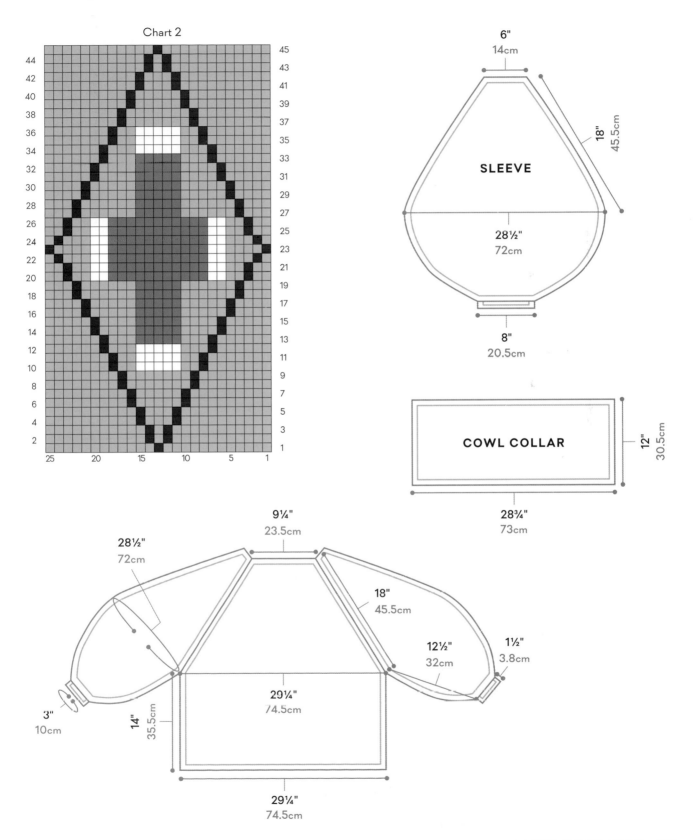

Chart 2

SLEEVE

6"
14cm

18"
45.5cm

28½"
72cm

8"
20.5cm

COWL COLLAR

12"
30.5cm

28¾"
73cm

9¼"
23.5cm

28½"
72cm

18"
45.5cm

12½"
32cm

1½"
3.8cm

3"
10cm

14"
35.5cm

29¼"
74.5cm

29¼"
74.5cm

VICTORY FAIR ISLE
pullover

With its beautiful fit and easy but intricate stitch work, this sweater is a new classic for your wardrobe. I am a big fan of traditional Fair Isle knitting, but I always try to kick it up a notch by mixing the treasured technique with other stitch patterns and textures, or by giving it nontraditional placement, as you can see here. Be warned, this piece is a major time investment and not for a novice knitter. There is Fair Isle color work (in this case, with lots of ends to work in) and the combination of the colors and stitch pattern is seriously exciting knitting.

reimagine it
Imagine omitting the fur on this piece and using a cabled or bobbled I-cord in its place. Instead of the Fair Isle pattern, make the V and sleeves in an easy stripe or a solid color.

SKILL LEVEL

TIME

SIZES

S (M, L), *shown in size M*

FINISHED MEASUREMENTS

Bust/lower edge circumference: 35 (40, 45)" [89 (101.5, 114)cm]

Length: 24½ (26½, 27¾)" [62 (67.5, 70.5)cm]

GAUGE

24 stitches and 32 rows = 4" (10cm) in stockinette stitch using size U.S. 6 (4mm) needles.

26 stitches and 30 rows = 4" (10cm) over Lattice pattern using size U.S. 6 (4mm) needles.

27 stitches and 27 rows = 4" (10cm) over Fair Isle pattern using size U.S. 6 (4mm) needles.

16 stitches = 4" (10cm) over stockinette stitch using size U.S. 10½ needles with fur yarn (row gauge not necessary)

Take time to check gauge.

MATERIALS

Rowan Felted Tweed (50% wool, 25% alpaca, 25% viscose), 1¾ oz (50g), 191 yd (175m); 6 (6, 7) balls of # 175 Cinnamon (A), 1 each of the following: #167 Maritime (B), #158 Pine (C), #153 Phantom (D), #178 Seasalter (E), #184 Celadon (F), #150 Rage (G), #161 Avocado (H), #154 Ginger (J), #177 Clay (L), #181 Mineral (M)

Prism Plume (100% nylon) 2.8 oz (79g), 45 yd (41m), 2 skeins of Denali

Size U.S. 4 (3.5mm) 16" (40.5cm) and 32" (81cm) circular needles

Size U.S. 6 (4mm) 16" (40.5cm) circular needles, or size needed to obtain gauge

Size U.S. 6 (4mm) 32" (81cm) circular needles, or size needed to obtain gauge

Size U.S. 10½ (6.5mm) 16" (40.5cm) circular needles

Stitch holders

25 stitch markers

Tapestry needle

Lattice Pattern

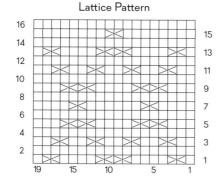

Stitch Key

☐ K on RS, P on WS
⊠ RT
⊠ LT
☐ Repeat

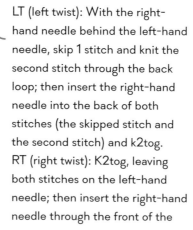

Pattern Stitches

LT (left twist): With the right-hand needle behind the left-hand needle, skip 1 stitch and knit the second stitch through the back loop; then insert the right-hand needle into the back of both stitches (the skipped stitch and the second stitch) and k2tog.

RT (right twist): K2tog, leaving both stitches on the left-hand needle; then insert the right-hand needle through the front of the first stitch just knitted together, and knit the first stitch again; then slip both stitches from the needle together.

Lattice Pattern
(multiple of 8 stitches + 2)
Row 1 (RS): K1, *LT, k4, RT; repeat from * to the last stitch, k1.
Row 2 and all WS rows: Purl.
Row 3: K2, *LT, k2, RT, k2; repeat from * to end.
Row 5: K3, *LT, RT, k4; repeat

from * to the last 7 stitches, LT, RT, k3.

Row 7: K4, *RT, k6; repeat from * to the last 4 stitches, k4.

Row 9: K3, *RT, LT, k4; repeat from * to the last 7 stitches, RT, LT, k3.

Row 11: K2, *RT, k2, LT, k2; repeat from *to end.

Row 13: K1, *RT, k4, LT; repeat from * to the last stitch, k1.

Row 15: K8, *LT, k6; repeat from * to the last 2 stitches, k2.

Row 16: Purl.

Repeat Rows 1–16 for pattern.

BACK

With A and 32" (81cm) smallest-size circular needle, cast on 114 (130, 146) stitches.

Work back and forth on the circular needle to make the hem. Beginning with a knit row, work 8 rows in stockinette stitch, ending with a WS row.

Purl 2 rows.

Change to the 32" (81cm) medium-size circular needle. Work 134 (150, 150) rows in Lattice pattern.

Shape Underarms

Next row (RS): Bind off 4 (5, 7) stitches, work in pattern to end.

Next row: Bind off 4 (5, 7) stitches, purl to end—106 (120, 132) stitches.

Place stitches on a holder.

FRONT

Note: Treat the Fair Isle V-neck panel as an intarsia shape, twisting yarns on the WS when changing from Lattice pattern to Fair Isle panel and back to Lattice pattern.

Work same as Back until 48 (64, 64) rows of Lattice pattern have been completed.

Fair Isle V Panel

Row 1 (RS): Work 57 (65, 73) stitches in Lattice pattern, drop yarn. With color of Row 1 of Fair Isle V chart, m1, drop yarn. Attach a new ball of A and work 57 (65, 73) stitches in Lattice pattern—115 (131, 147).

Row 2: Purl, keeping in patterns and colors as established.

Row 3: With A, work in Lattice pattern to 2 stitches from V, k2tog, drop yarn. With color(s) of next row of Fair Isle V chart, m1, k1, m1 in colors of chart, drop yarn(s). With A, ssk, work in Lattice pattern to end.

Row 4: Purl, keeping in colors as established.

Repeat rows 3 and 4, keeping patterns as established, until row 86 of Fair Isle V chart has been completed and piece measures same as the Back to the underarm shaping.

Shape Underarms

Row 87: Bind off 4 (5, 7) stitches, work in patterns as established to the end.

Row 88: Bind off 4 (5, 7) stitches, purl to end, keeping in patterns and colors as established—107 (121, 133) stitches. Place stitches on a holder.

SLEEVES (MAKE 2)

With A and 16" (40.5cm) smaller sized circular needle, cast on 49 (49, 65) stitches. Work back and forth on the circular needle to make the hem: Beginning with a knit row, work 8 rows in stockinette stitch, ending with a WS row. Purl 2 rows.

Change to 16" (40.5cm) medium sized circular needle.

Row 1 (RS): With A, k1, work 18 (18, 26) stitches of Lattice pattern, drop yarn. With color(s) of Sleeve charts, work 11 stitches of Sleeve chart. Attach a new ball of A, work 18 (18, 26) stitches of the Lattice pattern, k1.

Row 2: Purl, keeping in patterns and colors as established.

Repeat rows 1 and 2, working through 128 rows of Sleeve

chart and keeping in patterns as established.

At the same time, working increases into Lattice Pattern, increase every 6th row 18 (20, 16) times as follows:

Increase row (RS): K1, m1, work in patterns as established to the last stitch, m1, k1—85 (89, 97) stitches.

Work even in patterns until row 126 has been completed.

Row 127: Bind off 4 (5, 7) stitches, work in patterns as established to the end.

Row 128: Bind off 4 (5, 7)

stitches, purl to the end, keeping in patterns and colors as established—77 (79, 83) stitches. Place stitches on a holder.

YOKE

With RS facing, 32" (81cm) medium sized circular needle, and D, k77 (79, 83) Left Sleeve stitches, k107 (121, 133) Front stitches, k77 (79, 83) Right Sleeve stitches, and k106 (120, 132) Back stitches—367 (399, 431) stitches. Place marker and join for working in the round.

Preparation round (RS)

Size S: With B, k2, k2tog, k61, k2tog, k127, k2tog, k61, k2tog, [k26, k2tog] 3 times, k24—360 stitches.

Size M: With B, [k10, k2tog] twice, k45, m1, k15, m1, k111, m1, k24, m1, [k28, k2tog] 5 times, k30—396 stitches.

Size L: With B, k378 (to center back), m1, knit to end—432 stitches.

All sizes: Place a marker every 18 stitches, using 20 (22, 24) markers around.

Work Yoke Chart

Size L only: Work rounds 1–4 and 8–11 of Collar chart, then continue as for all sizes.

All sizes: Work 44 rounds of Yoke

chart, working all decreases as k2tog, and changing to shorter circular needle as necessary—100 (110, 120) stitches.

COLLAR

Remove all markers and shift stitches around the needle to begin the new round at the center back neck.

Sizes M and L only: With C, *k9 (10), k2tog; repeat from * around—100 (110) stitches.

All sizes: Place a marker every 10 stitches, using 10 (10, 11) markers around.

Work 43 rounds of Collar chart.

Make Hem

Remove markers and change to smaller circular needle.

With A, knit 1 round, purl 1 round, knit 8 rounds.

Bind off *very* loosely.

FINISHING

Weave in all the ends. Sew side, sleeve, and underarm seams. Sew collar, sleeve, and body hems to the WS. Block lightly.

Add Fur Trim to Body

With the largest size circular needle and fur yarn, cast on 280 (300, 320) stitches. Knit 1 row.

Bind off. With A, whipstitch (see page 171) the fur trim to the body of the sweater, outlining the entire Fair Isle section, following photographs.

Add Fur Trim to Sleeve Cuffs

With largest size circular needle and fur yarn, cast on 30 (30, 35) stitches. Knit 1 row. Bind off. With A, whipstitch the fur trim to the sleeve edge. Repeat for the second sleeve.

Front V Chart

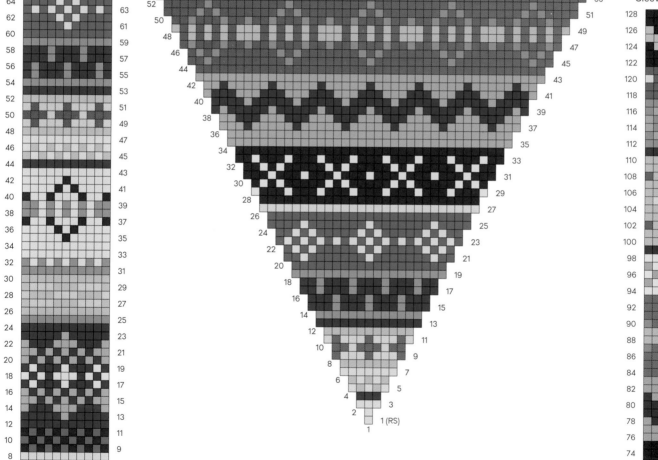

Sleeve Chart

Sleeve Chart (contir

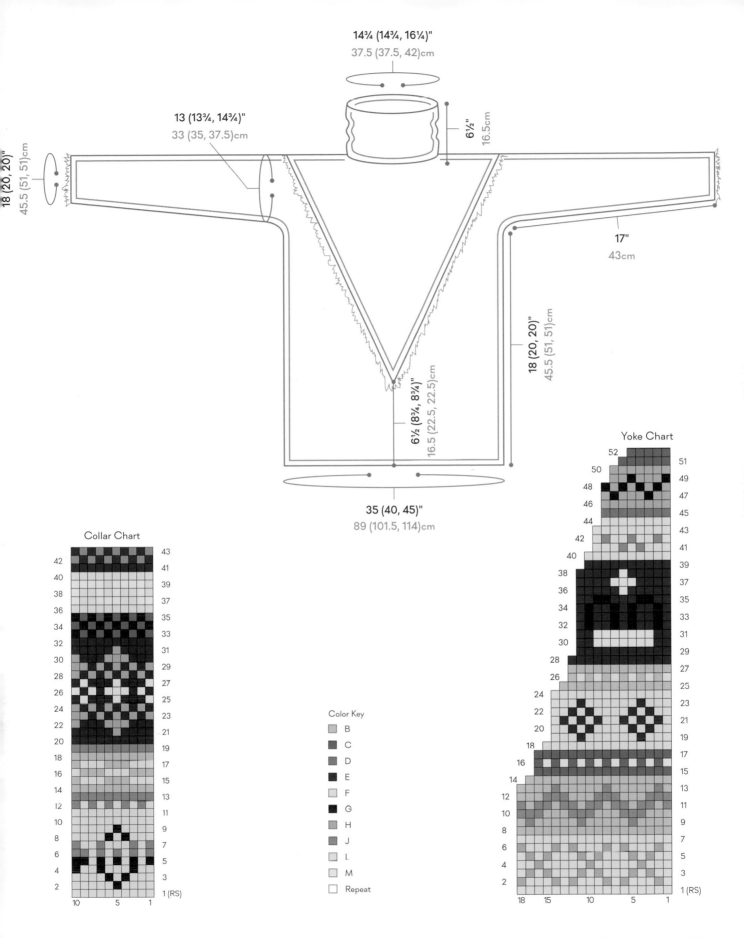

14¾ (14¾, 16¼)"
37.5 (37.5, 42)cm

13 (13¾, 14¾)"
33 (35, 37.5)cm

6½"
16.5cm

18 (20, 20)"
45.5 (51, 51)cm

17"
43cm

18 (20, 20)"
45.5 (51, 51)cm

6½ (8¾, 8¾)"
16.5 (22.5, 22.5)cm

35 (40, 45)"
89 (101.5, 114)cm

Collar Chart

Yoke Chart

Color Key
- B
- C
- D
- E
- F
- G
- H
- J
- L
- M
- Repeat

QUINTESSENTIAL CABLE
pullover

Peplums are always a favorite fashion silhouette. This design uses an easy cable rib pattern for a sleek fit, but the real interest here is threefold: the very unusual way the sleeves are made, the flap edging made in graduated short to long lengths on the bottom and sleeve edges, and the bold oversize rib collar that enhances the neck shaping and shoulder detail. The sleeve shaping is entirely innovative, so study the diagram for a better understanding of this new sleeve style technique. Also note the stunning side seaming.

reimagine it
You'll want to keep the unique sleeve construction and the flaps, so instead you may want to reimagine this pullover into a dress using a yarn with sequins or metallics. You can also leave off the collar for a sleek V-neck.

TIME

SIZES

S (M, L), *shown in size S*

FINISHED MEASUREMENTS

Bust: 32½ (37½, 41¼)" [82.5 (95, 105)cm]

Length above flap joining to shoulder: 20½ (23¾, 24¾)" [52 (60, 63)cm]

Sleeve length from wrist to underarm: 17¼ (18, 18¾)" [44 (45.5, 47.5)cm]

Note: This pattern is written for size S; the M and L sizes are achieved by using larger-sized needles.

Both stitch and row gauges are important.

GAUGES

For S: 26 stitches and 29 rows = 4" (10cm) on size U.S. 7 (4.5mm) needles in Cable and Rib pattern, slightly stretched

For M: 24 stitches and 26 rows = 4" (10cm) on size U.S. 8 (5mm) needles in Cable and Rib pattern, slightly stretched

For L: 22 stitches and 24 rows = 4" (10cm) on size U.S. 9 (5.5mm) needles in Cable and Rib pattern, slightly stretched

Take time to check gauge.

Notes: All decreases are made 1 stitch in from the edges as k2tog or p2tog as needed for continuity of pattern stitch. All increases are made 1 stitch in from the edges as m1k or m1p as needed for continuity of pattern stitch.

MATERIALS

Plymouth Select Merino Superwash (100% superwash fine merino wool), 3½ oz (100g), 218 yd (196m); 9 (10, 11) skeins of #0027 Caraway

Size U.S. 7 (8, 9) [4.5 (5, 5.5)mm] needles, or size needed to obtain gauge

Cable needle

Removable stitch markers

Stitch holders

Tapestry needle

Cable and Rib Pattern

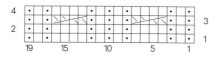

Stitch Key

☐ K on RS, P on WS

⊡ P on RS, K on WS

▱ 2/2 RC

☐ Repeat

Pattern Stitch

2/2 RC: Slip 2 stitches to the cn and hold in back, k2, k2 from cn.

Cable and Rib Pattern

Row 1 (RS): P1, k1, p1, *k4, [p1, k1] twice, p1; repeat from * to the last 7 stitches, k4, p1, k1, p1.

Row 2: K1, p1, k1, * p4, [k1, p1] twice, k1; repeat from * to the last 7 stitches, p4, k1, p1, k1.

Row 3: P1, k1, p1, 2/2 RC, [p1, k1] twice, p1; repeat from * to the last 7 stitches, 2/2 RC, p1, k1, p1.

Row 4: Repeat row 2.

Repeat rows 1–4 for Cable and Rib pattern.

BACK

First Flap

Cast on 19 stitches.

Repeat rows 1–4 of Cable and Rib

pattern 6 times, then work rows
1–3. Cut yarn and leave stitches
on needle.

Second Flap
Cast on 19 stitches.
Repeat rows 1–4 of Cable and Rib
pattern 7 times, then work rows
1–3. Cut yarn and leave stitches
on needle.

Third Flap
Cast on 19 stitches.
Repeat rows 1–4 of Cable and Rib
pattern 8 times, then work rows
1–3. Cut yarn and leave stitches
on needle.

Fourth Flap
Cast on 19 stitches.
Repeat rows 1–4 of Cable and Rib
pattern 9 times, then work rows
1–3. Cut yarn and leave stitches
on needle.

Fifth Flap
Work same as Third Flap.

Sixth Flap
Work same as Second Flap.

Seventh Flap
Work same as First Flap, but *do
not cut yarn*, turn.
Joining row (WS): K1,*p1, k1,
p4, [k1, p1] twice, k1, p4, k1, p1,
k2tog, repeat from * to the last 18

stitches, p1, k1, p4, [k1, p1] twice,
k1, p4, k1, p1 k1. Place a marker
at each end of the row—127
stitches.

Rows 1–32: Working in Cable
and Rib pattern, decrease 1
stitch each end of every RS row
15 times—97 stitches. Place a
marker at each end of row 31.
Rows 33–36: Work in pattern as
set. Place a marker at each end
of row 36.
Rows 37–50: Work in pattern,
increasing 1 stitch at each end
of every RS row 7 times—111
stitches.
Rows 51–82: Work in pattern,

increasing 1 stitch each end
of every 4th row 8 times—127
stitches.
Rows 83–86: Work even in
pattern.

Armhole Shaping
Rows 87 and 88: Bind off 8
stitches, work in pattern to
end—111 stitches.
Rows 89–94: Work in pattern,
decreasing 1 stitch at each end of
every RS row—105 stitches.**
Rows 95–148: Work even in
pattern.
Mark the center 41 stitches
for the back neck and place all
stitches on a holder.

FRONT

First Flap
Cast on 19 stitches.
Repeat rows 1–4 of Cable and Rib pattern 6 times, then work rows 1–3. Cut yarn and leave stitches on needle.

Second Flap
Cast on 19 stitches.
Repeat rows 1–4 of Cable and Rib pattern 5 times, then work rows 1–3. Cut yarn and leave stitches on needle.

Third Flap
Cast on 19 stitches.
Repeat rows 1–4 of Cable and Rib pattern 4 times, then work rows 1–3. Cut yarn and leave stitches on needle.

Fourth Flap
Cast on 19 stitches.
Repeat rows 1–4 of Cable and Rib pattern 3 times, then work rows 1–3. Cut yarn and leave stitches on needle.

Fifth Flap
Work same as Third Flap.

Sixth Flap
Work same as Second Flap.

Seventh Flap
Work same as First Flap, but *do not cut yarn,* turn.

Work from ** to ** of Back.
Row 95 (RS): Work in pattern over 52 stitches, join a second ball of yarn and bind off 1 stitch, continue in pattern over last 52 stitches.
Row 96: Working both sides at the same time, work even in pattern.
Rows 97–128: Work in pattern, decreasing 1 stitch at each neck edge every RS row 16 times—36 stitches each side.
Rows 129–144: Work in pattern, decreasing 1 stitch at each neck edge every 4th row 4 times—32 stitches each side.
Rows 145–148: Work even in pattern.
Place stitches on a holder.

SLEEVES (MAKE 2)

Flaps
Cast on 10 stitches.
Row 1 (RS): P1, k1, p1, k4, p1, k1, p1.
Row 2: K1, p1, k1, p4, k1, p1, k1.
Row 3: P1, k1, p1, 2/2 RC, p1, k1, p1.
Row 4: Repeat row 2.
Repeat rows 1–4 twice more, then work rows 1–3. Cut yarn and leave stitches on needle.
Make 2 more flaps the same as the first, but *do not cut yarn after the third flap,* turn.
Joining row (WS): K1,* p1, k1, p4, k1, p1, k2tog; repeat from * to the last 9 stitches, p1, k1, p4, k1, p1, k1—28 stitches. Place a marker at each end of this row to mark wrist.

Sleeve Shaping
Row 1 (increase row): Work in pattern to the last stitch, m1, p1.
Rows 2–119 (2–109, 2–105): Continue in pattern, repeating the increase row every 4th row 0 (5, 7) more times, then every 6th row 19 (14, 12) times—48 stitches.
Work 6 (8, 8) more rows in pattern, ending with a RS row.

Cap
Bind off 8 stitches, work in pattern to end—40 stitches.
Rows 1–6: Decrease 1 at the end of the next 3 RS rows—37 stitches.
Rows 7–49: Work 43 rows in pattern as established. Place a marker at each end of row 49 for the top of the sleeve.
Rows 50–92: Work 43 rows in pattern as established.
Rows 93–97: Increase 1 at the

p1, k1, p1. Leave the remaining stitches on the needle or place on a holder.

Row 2: K1, p1, k1, p4, k1, p1, k1.

Row 3: P1, k1, p1, k4, p1, k1, p1.

Row 4: Repeat row 2.

Repeat rows 1–4 twice, then rows 1–3.

Bind off.

*Join yarn to next stitch on a holder and work the next flap same as the first; repeat from * for the third flap.

COLLAR

Cast on 145 stitches.

Repeat rows 1–4 of Cable and Rib pattern 9 times.

Mark the center 41 stitches for the back neck. Bind off.

end of the next 3 RS rows—40 stitches.

Next row (WS): Cast on 8 stitches, work in pattern to end—48 stitches.

Sleeve Shaping

Work 6 (8, 8) rows even in pattern.

Row 1 (RS decrease row): Work in pattern to the last 3 stitches, decrease 1, p1.

Rows 2–115 (2–105, 2–101):

Repeat RS decrease row every 6th row 19 (14, 12) more times, then every 4th row 0 (5, 7) times—28 stitches.

Place a marker at each end of the last row for the wrist.

Flaps

Next Row (WS): K1,* P1, k1, p4, k1,p1, kfb; repeat from * to the last 9 stitches, p1, k1, p4, k1, p1, k1—30 stitches.

Row 1 (RS): P1, k1, p1, 2/2 RC,

WRIST BAND

(MAKE 2, OPTIONAL)

Cast on 10 stitches.

Row 1 (RS): P1, k1, p1, k4, p1, k1, p1.

Row 2: K1, p1, k1, p4, k1, p1, k1.

Row 3: P1, k1, p1, 2/2 RC, p1, k1, p1.

Row 4: K1, p1, k1, p4, k1, p1, k1.

Repeat rows 1–4, 14 more times. Bind off.

FINISHING

With the RS facing, join the 32 shoulder stitches of the Front and the Back using the 3-needle bind-off (see page 169), bind off the 41 Back neck stitches, use the 3-needle bind-off to join the remaining 32 shoulder stitches. Starting at right edge marker at the top of the Sleeve, weave a length of yarn over the ribs and under the cables to the left marker, then back again to the right marker. With RS together, sew the center sleeve seam. Set the sleeve cap into the armhole and adjust the gathers at the top using the photo as a guide. Sew optional wrist bands between wrist markers. Sew the sleeve seam from the Joining/dividing row markers to the underarm. Sew the side seams from the Joining row markers to the underarm, matching waist markers.

Pin the WS of the Collar to the RS of the neck opening, matching the center 41 stitches of the Collar to the back neck and the ends to the point of the V. Sew in place and tuck the seam to the WS.

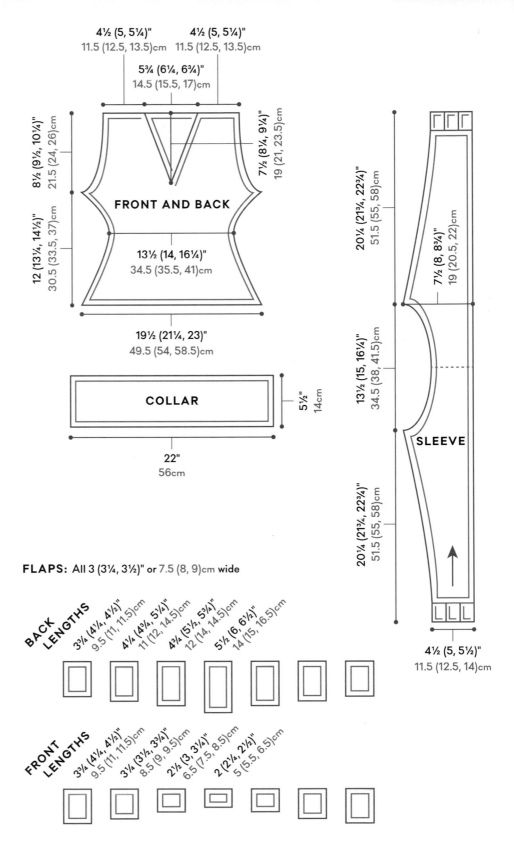

4½ (5, 5¼)"
11.5 (12.5, 13.5)cm   4½ (5, 5¼)"
11.5 (12.5, 13.5)cm

5¾ (6¼, 6¾)"
14.5 (15.5, 17)cm

FRONT AND BACK

8½ (9½, 10¼)"
21.5 (24, 26)cm

7½ (8¼, 9¼)"
19 (21, 23.5)cm

12 (13¼, 14½)"
30.5 (33.5, 37)cm

13½ (14, 16¼)"
34.5 (35.5, 41)cm

19½ (21¼, 23)"
49.5 (54, 58.5)cm

COLLAR

5½"
14cm

22"
56cm

20¼ (21¼, 22¾)"
51.5 (55, 58)cm

7½ (8, 8¾)"
19 (20.5, 22)cm

13½ (15, 16¼)"
34.5 (38, 41.5)cm

SLEEVE

20¼ (21¼, 22¾)"
51.5 (55, 58)cm

4½ (5, 5½)"
11.5 (12.5, 14)cm

FLAPS: All 3 (3¼, 3½)" or 7.5 (8, 9)cm wide

BACK LENGTHS
3¾ (4¼, 4½)"   4¼ (4¾, 5¼)"   4¾ (5½, 5¾)"   5½ (6, 6½)"
9.5 (11, 11.5)cm   11 (12, 14.5)cm   12 (14, 14.5)cm   14 (15, 16.5)cm

FRONT LENGTHS
3¾ (4¼, 4½)"   3¼ (3½, 3¾)"   2½ (3, 3¼)"   2 (2¼, 2½)"
9.5 (11, 11.5)cm   8.5 (9, 9.5)cm   6.5 (7.5, 8.5)cm   5 (5.5, 6.5)cm

EDGING
EPILOGUE
dress

Beautiful silk yarn with sparkling sequins and an asymmetrical design create a romantic silhouette perfect for an evening out. The neckline is sexy but wearable. The bold scalloped bottom edge flows into a quiet eyelet stitch to make the front and back. A double overlay of the scalloped edges along the top creates off-the-shoulder glamour. Three Swarovzki crystals are sewn at each scallop for a bit more glitz. The double overlay is used again for a wide shoulder strap across the left shoulder.

reimagine it
If you stay with the stunning yarn, consider lengthening the pattern to make it a dramatic dress or gown. Another way to go would be to use a cotton yarn (watch the gauge) for a more casual summer look.

SKILL LEVEL

TIME

SIZES

S (M, L), *shown in size M*

FINISHED MEASUREMENTS

Width: 15¾ (20¾, 26)" [40 (53, 66)cm]

Length from shoulder: 25¼ (27, 28½)" [64 (68.5, 72)cm]

Length from underarm: 18 (19, 20)" [45.5 (48.5, 51)cm]

GAUGE

18 stitches and 22 rows = 4" (10 cm) stockinette stitch on larger needles

Take time to check gauge.

MATERIALS

Tilli Tomas Disco Lights (100% silk), 3½ oz (100g), 225 yd (206m); 4 (5, 7) skeins in Ocean Spray

2 size U.S. 8 (5mm) 29" (73cm) circular needles, or size needed to obtain gauge

Size U.S. 6 (4.25mm) 29" (73cm) circular needle

Waste yarn or stitch holders

Tapestry needle

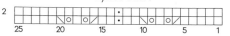

Scallop Chart

Eyelet Chart

Stitch Key

☐ K on RS, P on WS

▪ P on RS, K on WS

◌ Yarn over (yo)

◻ K2tog on RS, p2tog on WS

◹ Ssk on RS, p2tog tbl on WS

☐ Repeat

Scallop Pattern
(multiple of 23 + 2)

Row 1 (RS): K1, *k8, k2tog, yo, k1, p1, k1, yo, ssk, k8; repeat from * to the last stitch, k1.

Row 2: K1, *p7, p2tog tbl, p2, yo, k1, yo, p2, p2tog, p7; repeat from * to the last stitch, k1.

Row 3: K1, *k6, k2tog, k1, yo, k2, p1, k2, yo, k1, ssk, k6; repeat from * to the last stitch, k1.

Row 4: K1, *p5, p2tog tbl, p3, yo, p1, k1, p1, yo, p3, p2tog, p5; repeat from * to the last stitch, k1.

Row 5: K1, *k4, k2tog, p2, yo, k3, p1, k3, yo, k2, ssk, k4; repeat from

* to the last stitch, k1.

Row 6: K1, *p3, p2tog tbl, p4, yo, p2, k1, p2, yo, p4, p2tog, p3; repeat from * to the last stitch, k1.

Row 7: K1, *k2, k2tog, k3, yo, k4, p1, k4, yo, k3, ssk, k2; repeat from * to the last stitch, k1.

Row 8: K1, *p1, p2tog tbl, p5, yo, p3, k1, p3, yo, p5, p2tog, p1; repeat from * to the last stitch, k1.

Row 9: K1, *k2tog, k4, yo, k5, p1, k5, yo, k4, ssk; repeat from * to the last stitch, k1.

Row 10: K1, *p11, k1, p11; repeat from * to the last stitch, k1.

Row 11: K1, *k11, p1, k11; repeat from * to the last stitch, k1.

Row 12: Repeat row 10.

Repeat rows 1–12 for pattern.

Eyelet Pattern
(multiple of 23 + 2)

Row 1 (RS): K1, *k4, k2tog, yo, k1, yo, ssk, k2, p1, k2, k2tog, yo, k1, yo, ssk, k4; repeat from * to the last stitch, k1.

Row 2: K1, *p11, k1, p11; repeat from * to the last stitch, k1.

Repeat rows 1 and 2 for pattern.

FRONT

With larger needles, cast on 71 (94, 117) stitches.
Knit 2 rows.
Work rows 1–12 of Scallop pattern twice, then work rows 1–10 once more.

Work rows 1–2 of Eyelet pattern until piece measures 18 (19, 20)" [45.5 (48.5, 51)cm] from the beginning, ending with a RS row.

Armhole and Short Row Shaping
Row 1 (WS): Bind off 2 (2, 4) stitches; work in pattern as established to the last 5 stitches, w&t.
Row 2 and all RS rows: Work in pattern as established to end.
Rows 3 and 5: Bind off 1 stitch, work in pattern to 4 (5, 5) stitches before the last wrapped stitch, w&t.
Row 7: Work in pattern to 4 (5, 5) stitches before the last wrapped stitch, w&t.
Repeat row 7 every RS row 0 (1, 15) more times.
Next row (WS): Work in pattern to 3 (4, 4) stitches before the last wrapped stitch, w&t.
Repeat the last row every RS row 13 (14, 1) more times—8 (5, 8) stitches remain before the last wrapped stitch
Next row (RS): Knit to the last 10 stitches, lifting the wraps and working them together with the wrapped stitch, work 10 stitches in pattern—67 (90, 111).
Next row: Work 10 stitches in pattern, purl to end.
Next row: Knit to the last 10 stitches, work 10 stitches in pattern.

Next row: Work 10 stitches in pattern; purl to end.
Place all stitches on a holder.

BACK
Work the same as the Front to Armhole and Short Row Shaping, ending with a WS row.
Row 1 (RS): Bind off 2 (2, 4) stitches, work in pattern as established to the last 5 stitches, w&t.
Row 2 and all WS rows: Work in pattern as established to end.
Rows 3 and 5: Bind off 1 stitch, work in pattern to 4 (5, 5) stitches before the last wrapped stitch, w&t.
Row 7: Work in pattern to 4 (5, 5) stitches before the last wrapped stitch, w&t.
Repeat row 7 every RS row 0 (1, 15) more times.
Next row (WS): Work in pattern to 3 (4, 4) stitches before the last wrapped stitch, w&t.
Repeat the last row every RS row 13 (14, 1) more times—8 (5, 8) stitches remain before the last wrapped stitch.
Next row (WS): Purl to the last 10 stitches, lifting the wraps and working them together with the

wrapped stitch, work 10 stitches in pattern—67 (90, 111).

Next row: Work 10 stitches in pattern, knit to end.

Next row: Purl to the last 10 stitches, work 10 stitches in pattern.

Place all stitches on a holder.

LARGE SCALLOP BAND
(MAKE 2)

With larger needle, cast on 140 (186, 232) stitches.

Work Rows 1–11 of Scallop pattern.

Row 12: Purl, decreasing 26 stitches evenly across—114 (160, 206) stitches.

Place all stitches on a holder.

SHOULDER SCALLOP BAND

Cast on 71 (71, 94) stitches.

Work Rows 1–12 of Scallop pattern.

Work 8 rows in stockinette stitch.

Place all stitches on a spare needle.

Make a second Shoulder Scallop Band, working the same as the first to row 12.

With the RS facing up on both bands, place the first band behind the second band.

Next row (RS): *Using the smaller needle, knit 1 stitch from

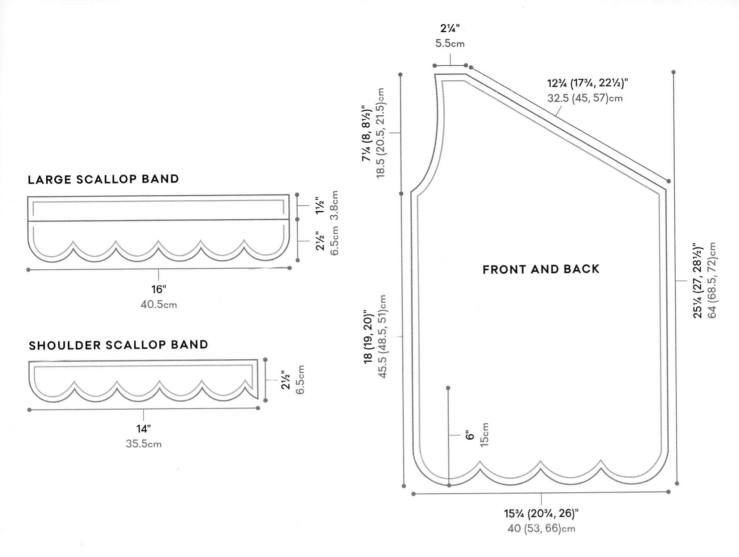

LARGE SCALLOP BAND

1½"
3.8cm

2½"
6.5cm

16"
40.5cm

SHOULDER SCALLOP BAND

2½"
6.5cm

14"
35.5cm

2¼"
5.5cm

12¾ (17¾, 22½)"
32.5 (45, 57)cm

7¼ (8, 8½)"
18.5 (20.5, 21.5)cm

FRONT AND BACK

25¼ (27, 28½)"
64 (68.5, 72)cm

18 (19, 20)"
45.5 (48.5, 51)cm

6"
15cm

15¾ (20¾, 26)"
40 (53, 66)cm

the second band together with 1 stitch from the right band; repeat from * to end—71 (71, 94) stitches.
Knit 5 rows. Bind off.

FINISHING

Place the shoulder stitches from the Front and Back (the 10 stitches worked in pattern) onto separate needles. Join the shoulder stitches using the 3-needle bind-off (see page 169). Place the remaining 114 (160, 206) stitches onto the larger needle, and the 114 (160, 206) stitches of one Large Scallop Band onto the smaller needle. With the RS facing up on both pieces, place the body needle inside the Large Scallop Band needle. Starting at the underam with the second larger needle, *knit 1 stitch from the band together with 1 stitch from the body; repeat from * around. Work 8 rows in stockinette stitch. Place the stitches of the second Large Scallop Band onto the larger needle. Using the smaller needle, join the second band the same as the first band. Work 5 rows in stockinette stitch. Bind off.

Armband

With the RS facing and smaller needle, starting at the underarm, pick up and k64 (70, 78) stitches evenly around the armhole. Knit 4 rows. Bind off knitwise on the WS.

Sew the side seams, starting at the uppermost row of the Scallop pattern, leaving slits at the lower edge. Leave the edges of the Large Scallop Bands unsewn.

Pin the ends of the Shoulder Scallop Band underneath the upper edges of the Front and Back, adjusting as necessary to fit. Sew in place. Weave in ends.

ABBREVIATIONS

Instructions for cables, bobbles and special increases/decreases are included with the pattern.

cn • cable needle

dpn • double-pointed needle

k • knit

kfb • knit in front and back of the same stitch

m1 • make 1 by lifting the bar between the last stitch and the next stitch, k1 tbl

m1p • make 1 by lifting the bar between the last stitch and the next stitch and p1 tbl

p • purl

p2tog tbl • purl 2 stitches together through the back loops

pbf • purl in back and front of the same stitch

pm • place marker

rnd • round

RS • right side

s2kp • slip 2 stitches as if to k2tog, k1, pass the 2 slipped stitches over the k1

s2pp • slip 2 stitches as if to p2tog, p1, pass the 2 slipped stitches over the p1

sk2p • slip 1 stitch knitwise, k2tog, pass the slipped stitch over the k2tog

sm • slip marker

ssk • [slip 1 knitwise] twice, insert LH needle through the front of the 2 slipped stitches and k2tog tbl

St st • stockinette stitch: knit on the RS, purl on the WS

tbl • through the back loop

tog • together

w&t • wrap and turn (see page 171)

WS • wrong side

wyib • with yarn in back

wyif • with yarn in front

yo   yarn over

KNITTING TECHNIQUES

3-NEEDLE BIND-OFF

With the right sides of the two pieces facing each other and the needles parallel, insert a third needle knitwise into the first stitch of each needle, wrap the yarn around the needle as if to knit, as shown. Knit these two stitches together and slip them off the needles. Repeat to end, binding off at the same time.

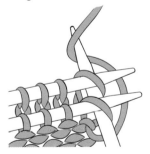

CABLE CAST-ON

With a slip knot on the left needle, insert the point of the right needle knitwise into the stitch on the left needle. Wrap the yarn around the right needle as if to knit. Draw the yarn through the first stitch to make a new stitch, but do not drop the stitch from the left needle. Transfer the new stitch to the left needle.

For each successive stitch to be cast on, insert the point of the right needle *between* the two stitches on the left needle. Wrap the yarn around the right needle as if to knit and pull the yarn through to make a new stitch, but again do not drop the stitch. Transfer the new stitch to the left needle. Repeat for the required number of stitches.

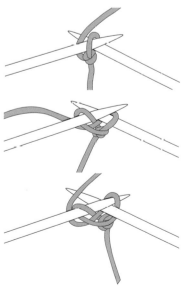

DUPLICATE STITCH

Thread a tapestry needle with the desired color. *Draw the needle from the back to the front at the base of the V of the knitted stitch to be covered. Bring the thread over the right-hand leg of the stitch, down into the stitch in the row above it, over the left-hand leg and back down into the base of the same stitch. Repeat from * working from right to left and bottom to top until the desired area is covered.

I-CORD

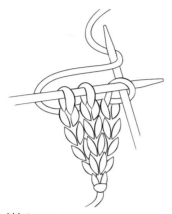

With two double-pointed needles, cast on 3 (4, 5) stitches. *Do not turn work. Slide the stitches to the other end of the needle, k3 (4, 5); repeat from * until cord measures desired length and fasten off.

INTARSIA

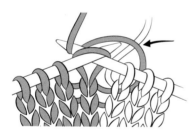

Step 1: On the knit side, drop the old color. Pick up the new color from under the old color and knit to the next color change.

Step 2: On the purl side, drop the old color. Pick up the new color from under the old color and purl to the next color change. Repeat these two steps.

KITCHENER STITCH

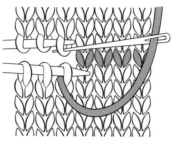

To set up: Thread a tapestry needle with a strand of yarn three to four times the length of the edge to be grafted together. Hold the working needles parallel to each other with the tips pointing in the same direction and the right sides facing up. Insert the tapestry needle purlwise into the first stitch of the front knitting needle, draw the yarn through, without dropping the stitch from the needle. Insert the tapestry needle knitwise into the first stitch on the back knitting needle, and draw the yarn through without dropping the stitch.

To graft: *Insert the tapestry needle knitwise into the first stitch on the front needle, and drop the stitch from the needle. Insert the tapestry needle purlwise into the next stitch on the front needle. Draw the yarn through and leave the stitch on the knitting needle. Insert the needle purlwise into the first stitch on the back needle.

Drop the stitch from the knitting needle. Insert the tapestry needle knitwise into the next stitch on the back needle, and draw the yarn through without dropping the stitch.* Repeat from * to * until all live stitches have been grafted.

COLOR STRANDING / FAIR ISLE

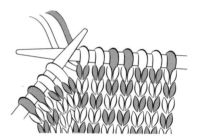

Holding colors left

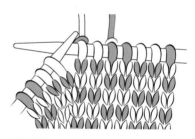

Holding colors right

Stranding one-handed: On the knit side, drop the working yarn. Bring the new color (now the working yarn) over the top of the dropped yarn and work to the next color change. Repeat these two steps when changing colors.

On the purl side, drop the working yarn. Bring the new color under the dropped yarn and work to the next color change. Repeat these two steps when changing colors.

Stranding two-handed: On the knit side, hold the working yarn in your right hand and the nonworking yarn in your left hand. Bring the working yarn over the top of the yarn in your left hand and knit with the right hand to the next color change.

The yarn in your right hand is now the nonworking yarn, the yarn in your left hand is the working yarn. Bring the working yarn under the nonworking yarn and knit with the left-hand needle to the next color change. Repeat these two steps when changing colors.

On the purl side, hold the working yarn in your right hand and the nonworking yarn in your left hand. Bring the working yarn over the top of the yarn in your left hand and purl with the right hand to the next color change.

The yarn in your right hand is now the nonworking yarn, the yarn in your left hand is the working yarn. Bring the working yarn under the nonworking yarn and purl with the left-hand needle to the next color change. Repeat these two steps when changing colors.

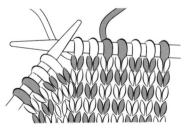

SLIP STITCH (CROCHET)

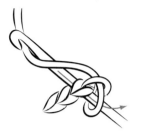

Insert the hook into a chain or other stitch, wrap the yarn around the hook, and then draw the yarn through both the stitch and the loop already on the hook.

WHIPSTITCH

Thread a strand of yarn into a tapestry needle. Holding two knitted pieces, stitch over the edge where the seams align to create small, evenly spaced diagonal stitches.

WRAP AND TURN (FOR SHORT ROWS)

Knit to the specified stitch, and with yarn in back, slip this stitch onto the right needle. Bring the yarn from back to front, wrapping the stitch.

Slip the same stitch back to the left needle.

Turn the work. Bring the yarn to the front or back (depending on whether you are knitting or purling) to complete the wrap. Finish working the row.

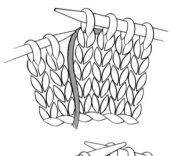

RESOURCES

Aslan Trends
8 Maple Street
Port Washington, NY 11050
(800) 314-8202
www.aslantrends.com

The BagSmith
24000 Mercantile Road, Suite 7
Beachwood, OH 44122
(888) 879-7224
www.bagsmith.com

Berroco, Inc.
1 Tupperware Drive, Suite 4
N. Smithfield, RI 02896-6815
(401) 769-1212
www.berroco.com

Blue Heron Yarns
8737 Brooks Drive, #108
Easton, MD 21601
(410) 819-0401
www.blueheronyarns.com

Blue Sky Alpacas, Inc.
P.O. Box 88
Cedar, MN 55011
(888) 460-8862
www.blueskyalpacas.com

Cascade Yarns
1224 Andover Park East
Tukwila, WA 98188
www.cascadeyarns.com

Crystal Palace
160 23rd Street
Richmond, CA 94804
www.straw.com

Fyberspates
Unit 1 + 6 Oxleaze Farm
Workshops
Broughton Poggs
Filkins Lechlade
Gloucestershire GL7 3RB
United Kingdom
+44 1367 850880
www.fyberspates.co.uk

HPKY (Hand Painted Knitting Yarns)
7 Tiffany Lynn Court
Wentzville, MO 63385
(636) 332-9931
www.hpkyllc.com

JHB Buttons
1955 South Quince Street
Denver, CO 80231
(800) 525-9007
www.buttons.com

Kollage Yarns
3591 Cahaba Beach Road
Birmingham, AL 35242
(888) 829-7758
www.kollageyarns.com

Lion Brand Yarn
34 West 15th Street
New York, NY 10011
www.lionbrand.com

Madelinetosh
7515 Benbrook Parkway
Benbrook, TX 76126
(817) 249-3066
www.madelinetosh.com

Plymouth Yarn Company, Inc.
500 Lafayette Street
Bristol, PA 19007
(215) 788-0459
www.plymouthyarn.com

Prism Yarns
3140 39th Avenue North
St. Petersburg, FL 33714
www.prismyarn.com

Rowan Yarns
Green Lane Mill
Holmfirth
West Yorkshire, England
HD9 2DX
+44 1484 681881
www.knitrowan.com

Skacel Schulana
(800) 255-1278
www.skacelknitting.com

Tahki Stacy Charles, Inc.
70–60 83rd Street, Building #12
Glendale, NY 11385
(718) 326-4433
www.tahkistacycharles.com

Tilli Tomas
(617) 524-3330
www.tillitomas.com

ACKNOWLEDGMENTS

This unconventional book required a publisher with courage, imagination, and foresight. That publisher is Potter Craft, an imprint of Penguin Random House, and I want to thank the entire team for their ongoing support and great work.

Many thanks to:

My editors Betty Wong, who made my vision a reality, and Caitlin Harpin, who skillfully and beautifully made it all come together.

Stephanie Huntwork, art director, for the beautiful look she created that was simply perfect for my designs.

Rose Callahan, photographer, whose talent and enthusiasm is elegantly expressed in these gorgeous photos, and her assistants Demetrius Fordham and Bowen Rodkey.

Meg Goldman, stylist, whose great sense of style led to a harmonious wardrobe that beautifully blended with my knitted garments, and assistant Tara Ferri for all her hard work.

Yuko, hair and makeup artist, who made our beautiful models, Sanita and Nadine, look even more gorgeous.

My intrepid team of knitters, who in this book truly outdid themselves, especially dealing with the reimagined and off-the-beaten-track designs that looked challenging, but eventually, when they understood the premise, admitted were not much more difficult to execute than traditional knitting.

My talented and "always there" knitters Nancy Henderson, Jo Brandon, Eileen Curry, Mary Taylor, and Dianne Weitzul, along with Sammi Sherwin, Eva Wilkins, Marla Fialkow, Dana Vessa, and Megan Hand. I cannot imagine a better group of talented people.

And to Eve Eng for easy-to-follow instructions.

My supportive friends Debbie Rufrano, Ashley Panaro, Emily Brenner, Christine Farrow, and Ryan Brandon.

Thank you as well to Cascade Yarns and to all the yarn manufacturers for their support and to Faryl Robin at Seychelles for the shoes, Karen Ko at K2o and Joan Goodman at Pono for their amazing jewelry, and to Jennifer Ouellette for the hats.

And last, but certainly not least, thank you to Melody Remillard and the entire staff of Grey Towers National Historic Site for their hospitality and for allowing us to photograph the pieces at this beautiful estate. If you're ever in the Milford, Pennsylvania, area you must visit this magnificent and historic wonder.

INDEX

ABOUT THE AUTHOR

Nicky Epstein is the beloved knitwear designer and best-selling author of numerous books, including *Knitting Block by Block, Knitting in Circles,* the Knitting on the Edge series, *Knitting on Top of the World,* and *Nicky Epstein's Knitted Flowers.* Must-haves in the libraries of designers and knitters alike, her award-winning knitting and crochet books range from highly original resource books to knitting/travel books to collections for Barbie and 18" dolls. She is a three-time winner of the National Independent Book Publisher's Award for Best Craft Book of the Year.

Her innovative and fashion-forward designs have appeared in every major knitwear magazine, in museum exhibits, and on television. She loves to share her expertise and enthusiasm for knitting with countless fans around the world and has traveled and taught throughout the United States and in England, Australia, New Zealand, Italy, Canada, Argentina, Uruguay, and France, gaining a loyal following. She hosts popular knitting tours and recently launched the Nicky Epstein Knitting Club. A line of her designs and videos can be found on her website: www.nickyepstein.com.

Nicky lives in New York City but is constantly on the go, sharing her love of knitting with a fun-loving army of fans.